商务英语专业中高职一体化系列教材
总主编 李德荣

Workplace Communication Skills

工作场所交流技能

主编／卢宁宁
副主编／刘嘉 李智玲

上海商贸职业教育集团 组织编写

立信会计出版社
LIXIN ACCOUNTING PUBLISHING HOUSE

图书在版编目(CIP)数据

工作场所交流技能＝Workplace Communication Skills：英汉对照／卢宁宁主编. —上海：立信会计出版社，2012.9
商务英语专业中高职一体化系列教材
ISBN 978-7-5429-3631-8

Ⅰ.①工… Ⅱ.①卢… Ⅲ.①英语—口语—高等职业教育—教材 Ⅳ.①H319.9

中国版本图书馆 CIP 数据核字(2012)第 187960 号

策划编辑	徐雪芬 张 寻
责任编辑	徐小霞 周 瑜
封面设计	周崇文

Workplace Communication Skills——工作场所交流技能

出版发行	立信会计出版社
地　　址	上海市中山西路 2230 号　邮政编码　200235
电　　话	(021)64411389　传　真　(021)64411325
网　　址	www.lixinaph.com　电子邮箱　lxaph@sh163.net
网上书店	www.shlx.net　电　话　(021)64411071
经　　销	各地新华书店
印　　刷	常熟市梅李印刷有限公司
开　　本	787 毫米×1092 毫米　1/16
印　　张	8.25
字　　数	208 千字
版　　次	2012 年 9 月第 1 版
印　　次	2015 年 6 月第 2 次
印　　数	3001—5100
书　　号	ISBN 978-7-5429-3631-8/H
定　　价	20.00 元

如有印订差错，请与本社联系调换

Perface 总 序

中国的企业正在向与国际接轨的现代企业转型。这一转型就宏观层面而言，是一种文化的转型。其成功与否，取决于能否借鉴世界上（尤其是发达国家和地区）已被证明为成功的企业管理文化。企业管理文化博大精深，至关重要。它大可涉及国计民生、社会安定、企业责任、管理风格，小可涉及计划安排、日常管理、服务态度、待人接物。这一文化是整个社会文化的一个重要组成部分，且直接影响人民生活。令人遗憾的是，对这一文化至今尚缺少应有的关注和倡导。

上海商贸职业教育集团根据国家经济发展战略和教育部构建现代职业教育体系的要求，从2009年起致力于各级各类职业教育协调发展的研究和中高职教育有效衔接的实践，完成了中高职教育定位正确、专业培养目标与职业岗位培养方向对接、学历证书与人力资源和社会保障局职业资格证书融通的《会计》、《市场营销/连锁经营管理》、《金融事务》、《国际商务》、《现代物流》、《应用艺术设计》、《酒店管理》和《商务英语》8个中高职教育专业教学方案。其中《商务英语》是基于国际化视野、有机融入企业文化、所有课程进一步突出能力标准的全新开发的专业教学方案。

《商务英语》专业教学方案致力于引进新的国际教育教学理念，从理论到操作层面对旧的课程设置和教学内容进行改革，使之既与国际接轨，同时又适合中国国情。该教学方案大力引进国外课程，解决英语学习和专业学习的矛盾，意在终结英语学习和专业学习"两张皮"的历史，并探索中高职教育如何实现有效衔接或在一体化的研究中取得积极的进展。项目论证的有关专家一致认为新方案从实际而非概念出发，借鉴发达国家成功经验，大胆创新，为中高职商务英语专业的发展，开创了值得努力探索和实践的新道路。

该专业教学方案配套教材计划开发12种，按教学进程需要，我们将以下8门课程列入首批编写，这些课程包括《企业与社会》、《电话交流技能》、《工作场所交流技能》、《工作文件写作》、《商务谈判》、《管理学基础》、《国际贸易》和《营销学基础》。这些教材以英语为载体，介绍先进的企业管理文化，同时具有语言教材的一些特点，使之适合中国学生学习。与传统教材相比，新教材具有下列特点。

1. 专业课程体现专业特色，迈出与国际接轨的步伐

以往的专业课程没有明确的规定和规范，各校根据自身的条件和情况开设，有的侧重外贸，有的侧重营销，也有的将重点放在开设一些单证、报关等实务课程上。新教材积极借鉴国外相关经验，从培养目标出发，以"能用英语从事商务活动"为教改基本思想，以英语应用能力和商务实践能力为重点，以求达到"知识型、发展型技能人才"的培养目标。把商务专业知识的学习与英语学习自然地融合在一起，让学生既学专业，又学英语，两者相辅相成，相得益彰。

2. 切实做到中高职课程衔接

以往中高职互不通气，各行其是，所开设的课程有相似，亦有重复，非常不利于专业建设。新教材对中高职课程进行了明确的界定，即使是同一门课程，对课程内容和教学方式也作了明确的区分，尤其是对"双语"、"全英语"的界定，保证了中高职课程的有效衔接。

3. 标准细化，便于操作

新教材对课程的知识和技能要求作了全新的诠释和详尽的规定，由浅入深，知行一体，经过一定的教学思想的提示，十分有利于课程的实施。在体例上，这套教材既是专业教材，又具有语言教材的特点。在介绍专业知识的同时，对专业知识的语言载体——包括词汇、句型、习惯用法、商务英语的特点等用注释、标示及各类练习等手段，让学生掌握并应用，提高英语水平。这一新的尝试，旨在努力改变以往商务英语专业存在的英语学习和专业学习"两张皮"的状况，开创一条专业学习与英语学习融合的新路。

4. 运用先进的教学理念

教材从内容到形式均为创新型教材，从教学内容到教学手段，既充分与国际接轨，同时又适合于中国学生，为国内首创。在专业知识介绍方面，内容上力求基础、实用，文字上力求简明、通俗，以适合职业教育的特点和学生现有的英语水平。

我国的职业教育与发达国家相比差距很大。这也使它具有较大的发展空间和创新空间。职业教育的发展需要更多的关注、关心和扶持。本套教材系新创，问题和不足在所难免，希望广大教师在使用中提出宝贵的修改意见，以使本套教材得到不断完善。

上海商贸职业教育集团常务副理事长

冯伟国

2012 年 8 月 12 日

Workplace Communication Skills

Foreword

前　言

　　2011 年 8 月 30 日教育部颁发的《关于推进中等和高等职业教育协调发展的指导意见》(教职成[2011] 9 号),是我国第一个指导中等和高等职业教育协调发展的专门的教育政策文件。在总结我国教育发展的基础上,文件全面、系统地提出了中高职协调发展的意见,从专业设置到专业教学标准、培养目标、课程标准、教学条件等方面提出了中高职课程衔接的具体意见。根据这一指导思想,上海商贸职教集团组织相关专家教授就商务英语等 8 个专业开展调研,并在调研基础上制定了中高职一体化的教学方案。为有效实施新的教学方案,上海商贸职业教育集团积极组织教材编写,这一册《工作场所交流技能》就是新编的教材之一,供中高职商务英语专业学生和有相同需求的相关专业(如国际贸易、国际营销、涉外旅游等)学生使用。

　　本教材分两个部分:第一部分提供不同场景的工作场所对话(共 45 个),内容涉及工作场所交流的各个方面,帮助学生获取大量的感性材料,又通过大量练习让学生巩固和运用所学的内容。第二部分介绍工作场所交流的各种专门技能,包括如何应用语言和非语言技能、如何加强团队交流、如何创造有利于交流的气氛、如何认识自己和他人、如何主持会议以及如何解决冲突等。希望学生通过本教材的学习,掌握用英语进行工作场所交流的基本技能,为今后用英语从事商务工作打下基础。目录中打有"＊"的单元供中职学生学习,其余单元供高职学生使用,但未学过打"＊"部分的高职学生,须学习本教材全部内容。

　　为帮助学生更好地使用本教材,提高教学效率,本教材在编写时吸取了许多语言教材的特点。首先,教材语言力求浅显易读,避免使用过于艰深难懂的句子和词汇。对于语言(包括专业)上的难点,教材提供较为详尽的注释,既可帮助学生弄懂教材内容,拓宽知识,也有利于他们自学;此外,种类丰富和大量的词汇、句型的练习,旨在帮助学生举一反三,更好、更熟练地掌握语言技能。本教材努力探索一条"一举两得"的新路,既能帮助学生学习专业知识,同时又可以有效提高学生英语水平。这种专业学习和语言学习的融合,也许应该成为我国商务英语专业课程建设的亮点和特色。

工作场所交流技能

在教学上,我们建议采取专业知识和语言技能并重的策略。知识固然重要,但作为知识的载体语言,其重要性再强调也不过分。所谓"皮之不存,毛将焉附",建议在教学过程中把握好两者之间的关系,强调学以致用,让学生有更多实践、演示和发挥的机会。教学进度则可根据学生的英语水平和接受能力等实际情况来确定,部分可采用双语教学。

本教材在编写过程中,得到了上海商贸职业教育集团和上海商学院高职学院的鼎力支持,在此表示感谢。本教材编写具体分工如下:刘嘉编写 Part 1 的第一单元和 Part 2 的第一、第二单元,王嘉艺编写 Part 1 的第二、第三单元,雷小青老师编写 Part 1 的第四单元和 Part 2 的第七单元,卢宁宁的编写 Part 1 的第五单元和 Part 2 的第八单元,李智玲的编写 Part 1 的第六、第七单元,石小卉老师编写 Part 2 的第四、第五、第六单元,宋玲琳老师编写 Part 2 的第三单元。

为方便教学,本书配有录音和习题参考答案,需要的读者可访问 www.lixinaph.com 获取。

编者对这项充满创新的教学改革工作虽然热情投入,但限于经验和水平,不当之处在所难免,欢迎使用本教材的广大师生提出修改意见,以便不断改进,精益求精。

编 者

2012 年 8 月

CONTENTS
目 录

Part 1　Workplace Conversations ·· 1

Unit 1　Greetings and Introductions (Conversations 1–8)* ·············· 3
Unit 2　Informing and Explaining (Conversations 9–16)* ················ 17
Unit 3　Making Requests (Conversations 17–24)* ························· 29
Unit 4　Resolving Conflicts (Conversations 25–30) ······················· 43
Unit 5　Exchanging Ideas (Conversations 31–35) ························· 55
Unit 6　Giving and Receiving Instructions (Conversations 36–40) ···· 66
Unit 7　Workplace Interview (Conversations 41–45) ····················· 77

Part 2　Workplace Communication Skills ·································· 87

Unit 1　Verbal and Nonverbal Skills (1)* ···································· 89
Unit 2　Verbal and Nonverbal Skills (2)* ···································· 93
Unit 3　Work Team Communication* ··· 98
Unit 4　Creating a Communication Climate ································· 101
Unit 5　Working Together: Understanding Yourself and Others (1) ···· 106
Unit 6　Working Together: Understanding Yourself and Others (2) ···· 110
Unit 7　Conducting Meetings ·· 114
Unit 8　Dealing with Conflict ·· 119

Part 1

Workplace Conversations

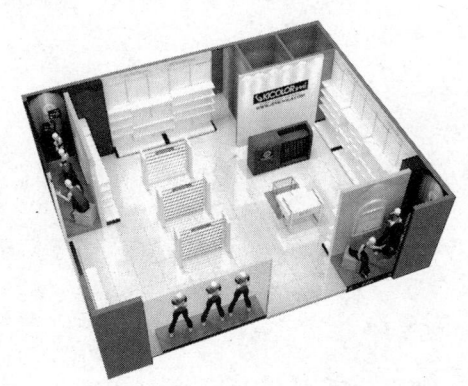

Part 1 Workplace Conversations

Unit 1 Greetings and Introductions

(Conversations 1 - 8) *

   A good first impression is one way of establishing a positive relationship with others. In business communication, proper clothing, a composed bearing and an authentic expression can help deliver a good first impression and a good beginning to a business deal. Greetings and self-introduction are the first step of giving a profound impression. Confucius once said that to be forever victorious in battles, you've got to know yourself as well as your enemy thoroughly. If people don't know their own company well, how can they work well and fully devote themselves to the business? A company that is able to let its employees feel proud and dedicated will surely win the trust of its customers. Therefore, employees should get familiar with their company, including its history, business scope, corporate culture and facilities.

Conversation 1

Words and Expressions
seem to be   看上去
in a hurry   很匆忙
in a minute   马上,很快
hold sb. up   耽搁某人
see you later 一会儿见

(*Tom and Mary are co-workers. They meet and greet each other in the office.*)

Mary: Good morning, Tom.
Tom: Hi, Mary.
Mary: You seem to be in a hurry.
Tom: Yes. I've got a meeting in a minute.
Mary: Okay. I won't hold you up then.
Tom: Right. I'll see you later.
Mary: See you.

Questions:
1. Who are talking in this conversation? Are they friends?
2. What are Mary and Tom talking about?
3. What is Tom going to do?
4. What does Mary say?
5. What do they do then?

Conversation 2

Words and Expressions
receptionist *n.* 接待员
make an appointment 预约
sales manager 销售经理
in the mean time 同时
visitor's book 来宾登记簿
conference room 会议室

(*Ann is the receptionist of the company. She is greeting Mr. Smith, a guest of Manager Mr. Hard.*)

Ann: Good morning, Sir. Welcome to our company. May I help you?
Smith: Good morning. I would like to see Mr. Hard.
Ann: Have you made an appointment[1]?
Smith: Yes, I've got an appointment with him at 9:30.
Ann: Can I have your name, please?
Smith: Tom Smith, the Sales Manager from ABC Company.
Ann: Let me see. Yes, Mr. Smith, we have been expecting you[2]. Please have a seat. I will call Mr. Hard at once.
Smith: Thank you.
Ann: Mr. Hard will be able to see you shortly. In the mean time, would you please sign the

visitor's book[3]?
Smith: OK.
Ann: Thank you. Please come with me, I will show you to the conference room.

Notes:

1. Have you made an appointment? 你有预约吗?
2. We have been expecting you. 我们在期待您的到来。
3. In the mean time, would you please sign the visitor's book? 同时请您在访客本上签名好吗?

Questions:
1. Who are talking in this conversation? Are they friends?
2. What are Ann and Mr. Smith talking about?
3. Did Mr. Smith have an appointment?
4. What did Ann do when she had confirmed Mr. Smith's identity?
5. What did Ann do after she contacted Mr. Hard?

Conversation 3

Words and Expressions
newcomer   n. 新员工
superior   n. 上司
graduate from   从……毕业
major   n. 专业
environmental engineering   环境工程
honored   a. 荣幸的
considerate   a. 体贴的, 考虑周到的

(*John is a newcomer in the company. He is introducing himself to his superior Lisa.*)
Lisa: Hello. Are you our new colleague, John?
John: Oh, yes. Lisa. May I introduce myself?
Lisa: OK. That's wonderful. Please.
John: Hello. I'm John. I will graduate from MIT this summer vacation[1]. My major is Environmental Engineering.
Lisa: Welcome to our company.

John: Thank you. I'm honored to work with you[2].
Lisa: By the way, everybody, John is a newcomer, so let's help him as far as we can[3].
John: You are so considerate.
Lisa: Whenever you have trouble, please let us know.

Notes:

1. I will graduate from MIT this summer vacation. 我今年夏天将从麻省理工大学毕业。MIT 系 Massachusetts Institute of Technology 的缩写。
2. I'm honored to work with you. 能和您一起工作我很荣幸。
3. Let's help him as far as we can. 我们尽全力帮助他吧。

Questions:
1. Who are talking in this conversation? Are they friends?
2. What are John and Lisa talking about?
3. What did John do at the beginning of the conversation?
4. What did you know about John?
5. What did Lisa say to the colleagues?
6. What's John's response to Lisa?
7. What's Lisa's attitude toward John?

Conversation 4

Words and Expressions
assistant *n.* 助理
secretary *n.* 秘书
be in charge of 负责
marketing research 市场调研部
assistant manager 副经理
sales division 销售部
make one's acquaintance 认识某人

(*Mr. Wang is a newcomer. The Manager of Human Resources Department Miss. Yang is introducing some colleagues to him.*)
Miss Yang: Let me introduce you to the people in the office.

Mr. Wang: Fine.
Miss Yang: Mr. Wang, this is my assistant, Jenny.
Mr. Wang: It's my pleasure to meet you, Jenny.
Miss Yang: Now, I'd like you to meet my secretary, Helen.
Helen: Pleased to meet you, Mr. Wang.
Mr. Wang: Nice to meet you. Call me Jack.
Paul: Very glad to work with you. I'm Paul, in charge of the office work[1]. If you've got any problem you can ask me.
Mr. Wang: Thank you, Paul. That's very kind of you.
Miss Yang: This is Tracy.
Tracy: Nice to see you. I'm the assistant manager of the Sales Division[2].
Emily: I'm Emily. I'm in charge of Marketing Research. I hope we can work well together.
Mr. Wang: It's nice to make your acquaintance[3]. I'll try my best to get into the team.

Notes:

1. I'm Paul, in charge of the office work. 我是保罗,负责办公室工作。
2. I am the assistant manager of the Sales Division. 我是销售部门的助理经理。
3. It's nice to make your acquaintance. 很高兴能和你认识。

Questions:

1. Who are talking in this conversation? Are they friends?
2. What are Mr. Wang and Miss Yang talking about?
3. Who is Jenny Miller?
4. What does Helen Smith do?
5. What do you know about Emily Brown?
6. What is the position of David Hard?

Conversation 5

Words and Expressions
banquet   *n.* 宴会
sort   *n.* 种类
Imp. & Exp. Corporation   进出口公司
be in charge of   负责
get in touch with   与……联系

Workplace Communication Skills 工作场所交流技能

> business scope　经营范围
> for your reference　供您参考

(*Mr. High and Mr. Li are invited to a banquet. They don't know each other. They introduce themselves to each other.*)

Mr. Li: Good evening. I don't think we've met. May I introduce myself? My name is Li Wei.
Mr. High: Hi, I'm Jacky High. Pleased to meet you, Mr. Li.
Mr. Li: Pleased to meet you, too. I work for Appolo Imp. & Exp. Corporation. Here's my card.
Mr. High: Thank you. What sort of work do you do at Appolo?
Mr. Li: I'm in charge of Marketing. At the back of my card is our business scope for your reference[1]. Mr. High, how can I get in touch with you?
Mr. High: Oh, yes. I'm from Stone's Company, Chicago. Here's my card.
Mr. Li: Thank you, I hope we can do some business in the near future, Mr. High.
Mr. High: Sure. I hope so, too.

Notes:

1. At the back of my card is our business scope for your reference. 我名片的背面是我们公司的经营范围供您参考。

Questions:
1. Who are talking in this conversation? Are they friends?
2. What are Mr. High and Mr. Li talking about?
3. Where did Mr. Li work?
4. What did Mr. Li do?
5. What did you know about Mr. High?
6. What did they say at the last of the conversation?

Conversation 6

> **Words and Expressions**
> appointment　*n.* 约会
> available　*a.* 在的, 可获得的

> elevator   n. 电梯
> employee   n. 员工，雇员
> be subject to   从属于
> draft a contract   起草合同
> interpretation   n. 口译
> introduce   v. 介绍

(*Jack is coming to meet Mary, the manager of Human Resources Department. The receptionist introduces the office of Mary. And then Mary introduces the responsibility of Jack.*)

Jack: Excuse me, could you show me the way to the Human Resources Department please? I am new here. I had an appointment with Mary.
Receptionist: I will call her at once. OK, she is available now. Please go to room 601.
Jack: Oh, thank you very much. But can you tell me where that room is?
Receptionist: It's the first room on the sixth floor. You can take the elevator over there[1].
Jack: All right. Thank you. Have a good day.
Jack: Good morning, I am the new employee and my name is Jack.
Mary: Good morning Jack. Nice to meet you. I am the Human Resources manager, Mary.
Jack: Nice to meet you too, Mary.
Mary: You do know that you are subject to the Sales Department, right[2]?
Jack: Yes, I know about that. So where can I start my work?
Mary: Well, your job involves drafting contracts and interpretation at meetings[3].
Jack: And at the present?
Mary: Tom will be your partner and he will introduce everything to you. He is coming.

Notes:

1. You can take the elevator over there. 你可以乘坐那边的电梯。
2. You do know that you are subject to the Sales Department, right? 你知道你在销售部门工作，是吗？
3. Your job involves drafting contracts and interpretation at meetings. 你的工作包括合同起草和会议翻译。

Questions:
1. Who are talking in this conversation? Are they friends?
2. What is Jack coming for?
3. Where is the office of Mary?

4. Which department does Jack work for?
5. What is the responsibility of Jack?
6. What should Jack do now?

Conversation 7

Words and Expressions
found   v. 建立
joint-venture   合资公司
leading   a. 领先的
manufacturer   n. 生产商
affiliate   n. 分公司
reside   v. 居住
head office   总部

(*Mr. Yang is introducing his company to his friend Mr. Wang.*)

Mr. Yang: Have you heard of our company before?
Mr. Wang: I heard about your company often. Your company is well-known all over the world. When was your company founded?
Mr. Yang: Our company was established in 1910 as the first joint-venture company with a western partner[1].
Mr. Wang: As I know, your company is one of the leading car manufacturers in China[2]. How many employees do you have?
Mr. Yang: We have about 50,000 employees including those working in our affiliate[3]. More than 2,000 travel all over the world, with about 1,000 residing abroad[4].
Mr. Wang: Well, I'm surprised to hear how huge your company is. Where is your head office?
Mr. Yang: It's in Shanghai.

 **Notes:**

1. Our company was established in 1910 as the first joint-venture company with a western partner. 我们公司建立于1910年,是第一家中西合资企业。
2. As I know, your company is one of the leading car manufacturers in China. 我知道,贵公司是中国汽车制造业的领头羊。
3. We have about 50,000 employees including those working in our affiliate. 包括分公司我们

大约有 5 万名员工。
4. More than 2,000 travel all over the world, with about 1,000 residing abroad. 我们公司有 2,000 多名员工往返于世界各地,还有大约 1,000 名员工在海外驻扎。

Questions:
1. Who are talking in this conversation? Are they friends?
2. What are Mr. Yang and Mr. Wang talking about?
3. Where does Mr. Yang work?
4. When was Mr. Yang's company founded?
5. What is the business of Mr. Yang's company?
6. How many employees are there in the company?
7. Where is the head office?

Conversation 8

Words and Expressions
Head of Administration 行政主管
PC. 电脑 (personal computer)
in-tray 收文篮
stationery cupboard 文具柜
photocopier n. 复印机
fax machine 传真机
rest room 休息室
showroom n. 陈列室
a range of 一系列
R & D workshop 研发车间

(*Ross is introducing the department facilities to Mike.*)
Ross: Are you Mike Green?
Mike: Yes.
Ross: I'm Jessica Ross. How do you do?
Mike: Hello. Pleased to meet you.
Ross: Welcome to ABC Company.
Mike: Thank you.
Ross: I'm the Head of Administration in the Marketing Department[1]. Our boss is Mr. Black. Let me show you the department.
Mike: Good.

Ross: This is the Marketing Department. This is my desk. Err ... that's Mr. Black's office. He's not here at the moment. And this is your desk; telephone, P. C., in-tray. This way please.
Mike: Thanks.
Ross: Over here is the stationery cupboard, papers, files, pencils, etc. Help yourself to what you need[2]. Here is the photocopier. And here is the fax machine.
Mike: OK.
Ross: The rest room is on our left. You can get water, tea or coffee at any time there as you like. Would you like a cup of coffee?
Mike: No, thanks.
Ross: This is the showroom. And here we have a range of products on display[3]. Come on; let's go to the R & D workshop.

Notes:

1. I'm the Head of Administration in the Marketing Department. 我是营销部的行政主管。
2. Help yourself to what you need. 要什么自己取。
3. And here we have a range of products on display. 这里陈列着一系列产品。

Questions:
1. Who are talking in this conversation? Are they friends?
2. What are Mike and Ross talking about?
3. Where is the position of Ross?
4. Who is the boss of them?
5. What does Ross show to Mike?

Key Expressions

I. Greeting and parting
1. Good morning/afternoon/evening.
2. How are you?
3. How do you do?
4. Nice/glad/pleased to meet you.
5. How are things? /How is everything? /How have you been?
6. See you (later). /So long.
7. Good-bye.

II. Introducing people
1. May I introduce myself?
2. Let me introduce myself.
3. Please allow me to introduce myself/my friend/my partner to you.

4. Have we been introduced?
5. Glad to meet you. /It's my pleasure to meet you.
6. I've heard your name many times before. /I have heard a great deal of you.
7. Come to meet my secretary. /I'd like you to meet my friend.
8. May I know your name?
9. It's with great pleasure that I introduce sb. to you.
10. I've been looking forward to seeing you.

III. Introducing the company and responsibilities
1. Our company was founded/established in 1998.
2. We have been in this business for 10 years.
3. We went public in 2006.
4. Our registered capital is 1 million yuan.
5. We mainly deal in import and export trade.
6. Our company is state-owned/privately-owned.

Workshop

I. Business vocabulary.
1. Give the English for the following business expressions.
   (1) 耽搁某人 _____
   (2) 销售经理 _____
   (3) 助理 _____
   (4) 市场调研部 _____
   (5) 经营范围 _____
   (6) 营销 _____
   (7) 起草合同 _____
   (8) 合资公司 _____
   (9) 总公司 _____
   (10) 行政主管 _____

2. Give the Chines version for the following.
   (1) in a hurry _____
   (2) make an appointment with _____
   (3) visitors' book _____
   (4) superior _____
   (5) conference room _____
   (6) graduate from _____
   (7) assistant manager _____
   (8) for your reference _____
   (9) affiliate _____
   (10) photocopier _____

3. Complete the sentences by using the words in the box.

seem to be	expect	make an appointment	graduate from
be in charge of	sort	be subject to	available
found	reside		

(1) I should like to get rid of the responsibility for this job, but there doesn't _____ anyone fit to hand over to.
(2) My son will _____ university.
(3) An experienced worker _____ the project.
(4) He _____ to finish the work by March.
(5) This plan is _____ your confirmation.
(6) TV sets are _____ in any department stores.
(7) Our guests _____ at the Grand Hotel.
(8) Please _____ with my secretary.
(9) All _____ of lamps are available in that shop.
(10) His theory is _____ on facts.

II. Listening practice.

1. Listen to the greetings and check the proper responses.
   (1) _____ a. No problem.
       _____ b. Not at all.
   (2) _____ a. How do you do?
       _____ b. Fine, thanks. And you?
   (3) _____ a. See you.
       _____ b. See you quickly.
   (4) _____ a. Thank you, take care.
       _____ b. You are more than welcome.
   (5) _____ a. Good night, grandma.
       _____ b. Good morning, grandma.

2. Listen to the statements and fill in the blanks below.

	Is living in ...	... years old	Works as ...	Is my ...
1. Robert Dias				
2. Anderson Brown				
3. Virginia Graham				
4. Daniel Vernon				
5. Paul Dias				

III. Complete the following conversations based on the Chinese given.

Conversation 1

F: Excuse me. Are you Mark Smith, the dean of the designing department?
M: Yes. Can I help you?
F: Good morning, Mr. Smith. I'm Frank, the new software designer.
M: Oh, hi. Nice to meet you. By the way, you can call me Mark.
F: _____（见到你我也很高兴）.
M: _____（我来带你熟悉一下办公室）. Here's your desk-phone, computer, and so on. Please sit down.
F: Thanks.
M: _____（这是你的工作说明）. Have a look at it.
F: All right, thank you.
M: _____（现在让我来告诉你在这里具体的工作职责）. You'll work in the third team, so you need to cooperate with six of other colleagues in the design of software of all kinds.
F: That's great.
M: _____（你就先看一下我们以前的档案吧）!

Conversation 2

W: Good morning. Can I help you?
V: Yes, _____（我与刘先生有个约会）.
W: Are you Mr. May?
V: Yes, that's right.
W: I'm afraid Mr. Liu is engaged at the moment. _____（您等一下好吗）?
V: Well. How long will it be?
W: About twenty minutes.
V: Oh, that's too long. I have another meeting at 11:00.
W: _____（副经理能办吗）?
V: No. I got in touch with Mr. Liu myself on the telephone yesterday and discussed details with him. I doubt if anyone else would know about the matter.
W: _____（您想与他另约个时间吗）?
V: All right. That's the only thing we can do at the moment. I'll come again on Friday. How about 10:30?
W: I'll ask for Mr. Liu's idea. Does he have your phone number?
V: Yes, _____（不过我可以把名片留下，以防他把我以前给他的名片丢了）.
W: Thank you, Mr. May. I'm sorry about the confusion but we'll see you on Friday.
V: Yes, thank you. Good-bye.

Conversation 3

T: As you've known, Mr. Brown is our managing director. He is responsible for running the company. He is assisted by four executive departments.

J: _____（我知道，有人事部、财务部、管理部和研发部）。
T: Exactly.
J: But I'm not very clear about their respective functions. So would you please give me some information?
T: _____（人事部主管员工，负责人员培训及人员管理工作）。The Finance Dept. as the name suggests, takes care of corporate finance and accounting. In terms of the Management Services Dept. it is led by Peter who is in charge of rationalization throughout the company. Finally, _____（研发部从事新产品的开发）。
J: I see. You mentioned five regions. Sorry, what are they?
T: _____（他们负责五个地区的日常管理工作）。
J: Do they also have sections under them?
T: Yes, Marketing Section and Technical Section.

IV. Role play.
1. You are the receptionist of a company. A client is coming to meet the manager of Sales Department. You will greet and accommodate the client.
2. You are the manager of the HR department. A new employee of the R&D Department is here to meet you. You will briefly introduce the company as well as his/her job.
3. You are at a business banquet. Try to introduce your company to a would-be client.

Unit 2 Informing and Explaining

(Conversations 9 – 16) *

Giving information and explanation is regularly done in all families, schools, companies and many other institutions. When a new employee comes to work in an organization, he has to be supplied with all sorts of necessary information so that he may gain a good understanding of his job. Good information exchange can help build an efficient work environment.

To provide explanation is to give reasons for any sort of undertaking. In order to be interpreted correctly, important explanation should always be delivered clearly and precisely, incorporating all relevant details currently on hand.

Conversation 9

Words and Expressions
green light 绿灯
hit the roof 火冒三丈
A/V equipment 视听器材
offer apologies 道歉
short time 短时间内
touch and go 难以预料的

(*Because of damaged equipment, Jim wants to cancel tomorrow's meeting.*)

Jim: I'm truly sorry about this, but we have to cancel tomorrow's meeting.

John: That can't be[1]! You know fully well how important it is. You gave me the green light just two days ago[2].

Jim: I know. But there's really nothing that can be done about it. The A/V equipment has been damaged and can't be fixed in such a short time.

John: Mr. Xia is going to hit the roof when he hears about it[3]. These negotiations are touch and go — this just might push them over the brink[4].

Jim: I'm going to tell all departments of the cancellation. It will be rescheduled with the client for Friday.

John: I'd better call the client again myself and offer my apologies.

Jim: Mr. Xia will be out of the office this afternoon. You'll have to tell him first.

John: I see. I'll go to his office at once.

Workplace Communication Skills 工作场所交流技能

 **Notes:**

1. That can't be! 那怎么行!
2. You gave me the green light just two days ago. 两天前你还说没问题的。
3. Mr. Xia is going to hit the roof when he hears about it. 夏先生知道了定会气得跳脚。
4. These negotiations are touch and go — this just might push them over the brink. 这些谈判本来就结果难料，这样一来可能就砸了。

Questions:

1. Who are talking in this conversation?
2. What's the relationship between them?
3. What are Jim and John talking about?
4. Will the meeting be cancelled tomorrow?
5. Is this meeting important?
6. What happened to the equipment?
7. How does John respond to the conversation?
8. Who is Mr. Xia?

Conversation 10

Words and Expressions
draw up   草拟
right away   立刻,马上
carry out   执行,实施
draft *n.*   草稿,草案
resolution   决议
anything else   还有什么事
try one's best to   努力做某事

(*Peter and Helen are arranging a business meeting; Peter tells Helen to inform every team member.*)

Peter: We are trying to arrange a meeting for next Tuesday. Please notify every member.
Helen: I'll do it right away.
Peter: Remember to prepare materials for everyone and put all the papers to be discussed into

this folder[1].
Helen: What about the drafts of resolutions[2]?
Peter: Put them into the folder, too.
Helen: I see. Anything else?
Peter: You need draw up a seating plan[3] and give each person a number[4].
Helen: I'll try my best to carry out the detailed preparation.

 **Notes:**

1. Remember to prepare … into this folder. 记得为每个人准备好材料,并把要讨论的文件放到这个文件夹里。
2. drafts of resolutions:决议草案。
3. draw up a seating plan:草拟一份座位表。
4. give each person a number:给每个人编号。

Questions:

1. Who are talking in this conversation?
2. What's the relationship between them?
3. What are Peter and Helen talking about?
4. When is the meeting?
5. What should Helen do?
6. According to Peter, what does draft of resolutions put in?
7. Who is responsible for drawing up a seating plan?
8. Does Helen need to number each person?

Conversation 11

Words and Expressions
interviewer　　*n.* 面试官
notification　　*n.* 通知
applicant　　*n.* 面试者
schedule　　*n.* 时间表
final decision　　最后的决定
look forward to　　期待(做某事)
notify　　*v.* 通知

Workplace Communication Skills 工作场所交流技能

(*The interview is almost finished, and the interviewer is telling the applicant to wait for the notification.*)

Interviewer: Well, that's all for the interview[1]. Thank you for your interest in this job.
Applicant: You are welcome. Thank you for taking time out of your busy schedule to interview me[2].
Interviewer: May I call you about our final decision?
Applicant: Yes, please. My telephone number is 2974-5328, and you can call me at any time in the daytime.
Interviewer: We will get in touch with you[3] by the end of next week.
Applicant: Great. I will look forward to hearing from you[4]. And do I need a second interview?
Interviewer: We'll notify you if necessary. Good-bye.
Applicant: Good-bye.

 Notes:

1. that's all for the interview: 面试到此结束。
2. Thank you for taking time out of your busy schedule to interview me. 非常感谢你在百忙中抽出时间来面试我。
3. get in touch with you: 和你保持联系。
4. I will look forward to hearing from you. 我期待着你的消息。

Questions:
1. Who are talking in this conversation?
2. What's relationship between them?
3. What is the main content about this conversation?
4. Does the applicant leave phone number?
5. When will interviewer contact the applicant?
6. Is the second interview necessary?

Conversation 12

Words and Expressions
specific   *a.* 具体的,专门的
training   *n.* 培训

decision　*n.* 决定
expect to　期待
get in touch with　与……联系
applicant　*n.* 申请人
reach　*v.* 取得联系
resume　*n.* 简历

(*The interview is almost finished, and the applicant is asking some questions . . .*)
Interviewer: Do you have any questions you want to ask?
Applicant: Yes, I'd like to know if there would be any future opportunities for specific training[1].
Interviewer: If necessary there will be. Any other questions?
Applicant: When will I know your decision?
Interviewer: We'll give you our decision in a few days. How can we get in touch with you?
Applicant: I can be reached at my office during work hours and at home in the evening. My office phone number and home phone number are in my resume.
Interviewer: Thank you for your interest in our company.
Applicant: Thank you, sir. I expect to hear from you as soon as possible.
Interviewer: Would you please let the next applicant come in on your way out[2]?
Applicant: All right. Goodbye.

 Notes:

1. I'd like to know if . . . specific training. 我想知道贵公司将来是否提供专门的培训机会。
2. Would you please let the next applicant come in on your way out? 你出去时请通知下一个应聘者进来。

Questions:
1. Who are talking in this conversation?
2. What questions does applicant ask?
3. How does the interviewer reply?
4. When will the applicant know the final decision?
5. How can the company contact the applicant?
6. What does the interviewer say before the applicant leaves?

Workplace Communication Skills 工作场所交流技能

Conversation 13

Words and Expressions
secretary   *n.* 秘书
avoid   *v.* 避免
rush hour   （交通）高峰时段
be held at   举行
plenty of   大量的
on time   准时

(*Susan is calling Mr. White. She informs the changed meeting time and explains the reasons.*)
Susan: Hello, may I speak to Mr. White?
White: Hello. This is White speaking.
Susan: I'm Susan, the secretary of the Overseas Engineering Company[1]. I'm calling to inform you of the time for the next meeting. The meeting will be held at 10:00 o'clock next Monday.
White: 10:00 o'clock? But my secretary told me that we would have a meeting at 8:30 a.m.
Susan: Sorry. We've changed the time to avoid the rush hour[2]. So we both have plenty of time to get there.
White: OK. I think I'll get there on time.

 Notes:

1. the secretary of the Overseas Engineering Company：海外工程公司的秘书。
2. We've changed the time to avoid the rush hour. 为避免交通高峰，我们改变了时间。

Questions:
1. What is Susan's position?
2. Can you guess Mr. White's position?
3. What company does Susan work for?
4. What's the reaction of Mr. White when he learns the change of the meeting time?
5. What's the reason for the change of the meeting time?
6. Will Mr. White ~~get to~~ the place on time?

Conversation 14

Words and Expressions
gathering *n.* 聚会
prepare *v.* 准备
extra work 额外的工作
convenient *a.* 方便
suit *v.* 适合

(*Antony is calling Tom and tells him why the arrangement is changed.*)
Antony: Is that you, Tom?
Tom: Yes, speaking.
Antony: I'm afraid that we must change the time of our gathering.
Tom: Why? We've prepared everything and we are just waiting for you.
Antony: My boss wants me to do some extra work. I'll have to stay in the office and I don't know when I'll finish it.
Tom: Will it be convenient if we postpone the gathering to 7:00 tomorrow evening?
Antony: I think that would suit me better.
Tom: So that's set[1]. At 7:00 tomorrow evening.
Antony: All right.

 Notes:

1. So that's set. 那就这样定了。

Questions:
1. Why does Antony call Tom?
2. What is Tom doing when Antony calls him?
3. Why can't Antony go to the gathering?
4. Does Antony know when he can finish the extra work?
5. What time does Tom suggest for gathering?
6. Does the new time arrangement suit Antony?

Conversation 15

> **Words and Expressions**
> pity   *n.* 遗憾
> tied up   忙碌的
> business matter   生意上的事情
> talk with   与……谈话
> cooperation   *n.* 合作
> worry   *v.* 担心
> good luck   祝你好运

(*Antony is calling Tom and tells him why the arrangement is changed.*)

Mr. Wang: Mr. Black. I'm afraid I won't be able to keep my appointment at 8:00 o'clock tomorrow.
Mr. Black: That's a pity. Do you think we can make it sometime next week[1]?
Mr. Wang: I'm afraid I'm tied up during these three months[2]. I'll be in Canada.
Mr. Black: You can call me when you are free.
Mr. Wang: I will. But for all business matter you can talk with my colleague, Miss Liu. She'll be glad to work with you.
Mr. Black: No problem.
Mr. Wang: I hope you will have a good cooperation.
Mr. Black: Don't worry about that. Good luck in Canada.

Notes:

1. Do you think we can make it sometime next week? 你觉得我们可不可以下周找个时间？
2. I'm afraid I'm tied up during these three months. 恐怕最近3个月我都抽不出时间来。

Questions:
1. Is Mr. Wang able to keep his appointment with Mr. Black?
2. Why is Mr. Wang unable to meet Mr. Black?
3. Where will Mr. Wang be during these three months?
4. Who can Mr. Black talk to for business matters?
5. Who is Miss Liu?
6. Is Mr. Black happy with the arrangement?

Conversation 16

> **Words and Expressions**
> hospitalize   v. 入医院治疗，住院
> heart disease   心脏病
> serious   a. 严重的
> recovery   n. （病情）恢复
> look forward to   期待做某事
> regards   n. 问候
> nuisance   n. 令人讨厌的东西

(*Mr. Norris is in the hospital now. Jimmy is telling Mike the appointment is canceled.*)

Jimmy: Hi, Mike. This is Jimmy of ABC Company.
Mike: Oh, Hi, Jimmy. How's it going?
Jimmy: Not bad. Thanks. I'm calling to tell you that our director, Mr. Norris, has been hospitalized because of a heart disease[1]. He has to cancel his appointment with you.
Mike: I'm sorry to hear that. Is it serious?
Jimmy: No, thank you. He hopes he can make a new appointment with you after his recovery[2].
Mike: I'll be looking forward to hearing the good news of his recovery.
Jimmy: He feels very sorry to be a nuisance[3].
Mike: It's all right. Please send my regards to him[4].
Jimmy: I will. Thank you so much.

Notes:

1. I'm calling to tell you that our director, Mr. Norris, has been hospitalized because of a heart disease. 我打电话是要告诉你，我们主任诺里斯先生因心脏病住院了。
2. He hopes he can make a new appointment with you after his recovery. 他希望康复后再约见你。
3. He feels very sorry to be a nuisance. 他非常抱歉不能履约。
4. Please send my regards to him. 请代我向他问候。

Questions:
1. Why does Jimmy make this call?
2. What happened to Mr. Norris?

3. What does Mr. Norris wish to do after his recovery?
4. What's the relationship between Jimmy and Mr. Norris?
5. Will Mike be happy to see Mr. Morris after his recovery?

Key Expressions

I. Expressing gratitude
1. Thank you/Thanks very much/Thanks a lot.
2. Thank you for ...
3. It's very/so kind of you ...
4. I'm so grateful that ...

II. Responding to expressions of gratitude
1. You're welcome.
2. It's my pleasure/With pleasure.
3. No worries.
4. I'm glad you like them.

III. Apologizing to sb.
1. I'm terribly sorry.
2. I'd like to apologize for ...
3. I must apologize to you for ...
4. Please pardon/forgive me.
5. I'm sorry to tell your that ...
6. I'm afraid that ...

IV. Asking about plans
1. What's your plan for ...?
2. Where do you want to go?
3. Have you decided ...?
4. Do you plan to go by ...?
5. You could visit ...

V. Talking about our own plans
1. I intend to do some traveling during ...
2. I think I want to go to ...
3. Let's go by ...
4. I plan/I wish to go to ...
5. We're going to ...
6. We will see/visit ...

Workshop

I. Business vocabulary.
1. Give the English for the following business expressions.
   (1) 火冒三丈 _____

(2) 道歉 _____
(3) 安排会议 _____
(4) 执行，实施 _____
(5) 期待做某事 _____
(6) 具体培训 _____
(7) 高峰期 _____
(8) 忙碌的 _____
(9) 恢复后 _____
(10) 代我问好 _____

2. Give the Chinese for the following business expressions.
   (1) fixed on _____
   (2) push over _____
   (3) draw up _____
   (4) right away _____
   (5) take time out of ... _____
   (6) be held at _____
   (7) extra work _____
   (8) cooperate happily _____
   (9) appointment with sb. _____
   (10) be sorry to be a nuisance _____

3. Complete the sentences by using the words in the box.

   | hit the roof | reached | be convenient | appointment | recovers |
   | prepare for | tied up | nuisance | change | rush hour |

   (1) Mr. Xia is going to _____ when he hears about it.
   (2) Remember to _____ materials _____ everyone and put all the papers to be discussed into this folder.
   (3) I can be _____ at my office during work hours and at home in the evening.
   (4) I'm afraid I'm _____ _____ during these three months.
   (5) Will it _____ _____ if we have a date at 7:00 tomorrow evening?
   (6) He feels very sorry to be a _____.
   (7) I won't be able to keep my _____ at 8:00 o'clock tomorrow.
   (8) I'm afraid that we must _____ the time of the date.
   (9) He hopes that the appointment will be held after he _____.
   (10) We've changed the time to avoid the _____ _____.

II. Complete the following conversations based on the Chinese given.

Conversation 1
Joe: We are planning to _____ (安排一次会议) for next Monday.
Tracy: I'll prepare it right now.

Joe: Remember to prepare materials for everyone and put all the papers to be discussed into this folder.
Tracy: _____（决议草案怎么办）?
Joe: Put it into the folder, too.
Tracy: I see. Anything else?
Joe: You still need to _____（草拟一份座位表）.
Tracy: I'll _____（尽力）make preparations for the details.

Conversation 2

Manager: Any questions you want to ask?
Mark: Yes, I'd like to know if there would be any future chances for _____（专门培训）.
Manager: If necessary there will be.
Mark: _____（何时我能知道结果）?
Manager: We'll give you our decision in a few days. _____（怎样才能联系到你）?
Mark: My mobile phone number and home number are in my resume.
Manager: _____（非常感谢你对我公司感兴趣）.
Mark: Thank you, sir. I _____（期待着）hear from you as soon as possible.

Conversation 3

Tom: Hello, Sammy. This is Tom of Johnson Company.
Sammy: Oh, Hello, Tom. How's it going?
Tom: Not bad. Thanks. I'm calling to tell you that our supervisor, Mr. Henry, _____（腿断住院了）and has to cancel his appointment with you.
Sammy: I'm sorry to hear that. Is it serious?
Tommy: No, thank you. He hopes that the appointment _____（康复后再约见你）.
Sammy: _____（我期待他的好消息）. Please send my regards to him.
Tom: I will. Thank you so much.

III. Role Play.

1. You are a senior account manager of an IT company. A major client suddenly comes to meet you and wants to discuss a new order with you, so you have to cancel a previous appointment with the manager of the Technology Department.
2. You are applying for a position in a state-owned company. During the interview with the manager of the HR Department, you are required to explain why you want to join this company.

Unit 3 Making Requests

(Conversations 17 – 24) *

To make a request is to ask for something. A request is not an order or command. Upon receiving a request, a person may choose either to meet or not to meet it. One may also choose to discuss it. Sometimes discussing a request might lead better ideas than the original request. In the workplace, a request may come from either the leader or a team member. Regardless of where it comes from, a request is invariably considered and responded to.

Conversation 17

Words and Expressions
file   *n.* 文件,文档
sales representative   销售代表
amazing   *a.* 令人惊讶的
job advancement   晋升职位
position   *n.* 职位空缺
responsible   *a.* 负责
entail   *v.* 涉及
perfect   *a.* 完美的
candidate   *n.* 人选
application   *n.* 申请
procedures   *n.* 程序

(*Cole and Anne are in the office, and Cole is proposing a promotion request to Anne ...*)
Anne: Hi, Cole. What can I do for you?
Cole: If you have a few minutes, I'd like to talk to you about my future at this company.
Anne: Sure, have a seat.
Cole: Thanks.
Anne: Let me look at your file. How long have you worked for us now?
Cole: I've worked here as a sales representative for about a year now.
Anne: One year already? It's amazing how time flies like that[1]. Are you enjoying your job?
Cole: Yes, but I'd like to have a chance at job advancement.
Anne: I see. What job did you have in mind?

Cole: Well, I've noticed there is a position available as a sales manager[2].

Anne: Do you understand what duties that job would entail?

Cole: Yes. I would be directly responsible for all of the sales representatives in my department. I assume there'd be more meetings, paperwork, and other responsibilities, too[3].

Anne: That's right. Do you have any experience in management?

Cole: Yes. In fact if you look at my resume, you can see that I was a manager before I started this job.

Anne: Well, I think you'd be the perfect candidate for the position[4]. However, according to the company policy, you'll still have to go through the formal application procedures[5] though, so fill this application form in and I'll call you in for an interview next week.

Cole: OK. Thanks for your support.

Notes:

1. It's amazing how time flies like that. 时间过得真快啊。
2. I've noticed there is a position available as a sales manager. 我注意到有个销售经理的职位空缺。
3. I assume there'd be more meetings, paperwork, and other responsibilities, too. 我想还会有更多的会议、文字工作和其他方面的责任。
4. I think you'd be the perfect candidate for the position. 我觉得你是这个职位的最佳人选。
5. according to the company policy, you'll still have to go through the formal application procedures：按照公司规定，你还是要走一下正式的申请程序。

Questions:

1. Why does Cole want to talk to Ann?
2. How long has Cole worked for the company?
3. What's Cole's present position?
4. What position does Cole want?
5. Has Cole worked as a manager before?
6. How does Anne think of Cole's request?

Conversation 18

Words and Expressions
salary *n.* 工资
rent *n.* 房租，租金
propose *v.* 提议

> take on　承担
> extra responsibilities　额外的责任
> scheduling　*n.*（人员、日程等）安排
> reasonable　*a.* 合理的
> cover a shift　顶班工作

(*Sue is explaining to Brown why she asks for a rise in salary.*)
Sue: Could we possibly discuss my salary sometime?
Brown: Sure.
Sue: First of all, I want you to know that I really like working for this company. Do you think I'm doing a good job here?
Brown: Well, you are a very hard worker.
Sue: The problem is, my salary just isn't enough to live on, even for food and rent.
Brown: What do you propose then?
Sue: I really want a 5% raise[1].
Brown: That's quite a bit[2]. If I give you a rise, I have to give everyone a rise.
Sue: Listen, if you pay me more, I'll take on some extra responsibilities[3].
Brown: That sounds reasonable. How about this, from now on, you will be responsible for scheduling. That means if you can't find someone to cover a shift, you'll have to do it[4].
Sue: That sounds good to me. I really appreciate it.

Notes:

1. I really want a 5% raise. 我想加薪 5%。
2. That's quite a bit. 那可有点多。
3. I'll take on extra responsibilities. 我会承担更多的工作。
4. That means that if you can't find someone to cover a shift, you'll have to do it. 那意味着如果你找不到人顶班，你得自己做。

Questions:

1. What are Sue and Brown discussing?
2. What's the possible relationship between Sue and Brown?
3. Does Brown think Sue works hard?
4. What problem does Sue have?
5. How does Brown respond to Sue's request of a pay rise?
6. What does Sue agree to do to have a pay rise?
7. What agreement do they reach in the end?

Conversation 19

Words and Expressions
unit price 单价
man-made *a.* 手工制作的
straw mattress 草席垫子
steady demand 稳定的需求
superior *a.* 优越的,优良的
transaction *n.* 交易,买卖
trial order 试订购
promote *v.* 促进

(*Jane and Joe are discussing the unit price for the hand-made straw mattress.*)
Jane: All right. Shall we get down to the price now[1]?
Joe: No problem. Our unit price for the hand-made straw mattress is $10 per piece.
Jane: I think the price is a little bit too high; can you give us a discount?
Joe: You know our product has a steady demand in the market[2] because of its superior quality. Our price is quite reasonable. If you place more than 1,000 pieces, we'll give you a 3% discount.
Jane: Well since this is the first transaction between us, we'd like to place a trial order of 1,000 pieces to promote our trade relationships[3].
Joe: Good.

 Notes:

1. Shall we get down to the price now? 我们可以讨论价格了吗?
2. a steady demand in the market: 稳定的市场需求。
3. We'd like to place a trial order of 1,000 pieces to promote our trade relationships. 我们想试订购 1,000 件产品以促进我们之间的贸易关系。

Questions:
1. What are Jane and Joe talking about?
2. What product does Jane want to buy from Joe?
3. What's the unit price Joe offers?
4. How does Jane think of this unit price? What does she ask for?

5. How does Joe respond to Jane's request?
6. Is there a deal made between Jane and Joe?

Conversation 20

Words and Expressions
depend on 依靠
settle *v.* 解决
reduce price 降价
merely *ad.* 仅仅
rough *a.* 粗略的,大概的
extent *n.* 程度
chemical fertilizers 化肥
supply *n.* 供应
exceed *v.* 超过
be apt to 有……倾向的

(*In order to conclude the transaction, Black and White are discussing the order.*)
Black: The size of our order depends greatly on the prices. Let's settle that matter first[1].
White: Well, as I've said, if your order is large enough, we're ready to reduce our prices by 2 percent.
Black: When I say your prices are much too high, I don't mean they are higher merely by 2 or 3 percent[2].
White: How much do you mean then? Can you give me a rough idea[3]?
Black: To have this business concluded, I should say a reduction of at least 10 percent would help.
White: Impossible. How can you expect us to make a reduction to that extent[4]?
Black: I think you are as well-informed as I am about the market for chemical fertilizers. It's unnecessary for me to point out that supply exceeds demand at present and that this situation is apt to continue for a long time yet[5]. May I suggest that you call your client to confirm that?
White: Very well, I will.

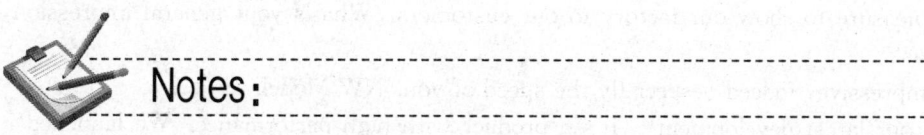

Notes:

1. Let's settle that matter first. 让我们先解决那个问题吧。

2. I don't mean they are higher merely by 2 or 3 percent. 我的意思并不是说它们仅高出 2 或 3 个百分点。
3. Can you give me a rough idea? 你能不能说一个大概的数字？
4. How can you expect us to make a reduction to that extent? 你怎么能要求我们给那么大的折扣呢？
5. This situation is apt to continue for a long time yet. 这种情况还要延续很长一段时间。

Questions：
1. According to Black, what does the size of order depend on?
2. What discount does White offer for a large order?
3. Does Black accept the offer of 2 percent discount?
4. What request does Black make concerning the price?
5. What are the reasons Black give for his request?
6. What does White think of Black's request?

Conversation 21

Words and Expressions
printed *a.* 印刷的
range *n.* 范围
general impression 总体印象
impressive *a.* 令人印象深刻的
high performance 高性能
launch *v.* （产品）投放市场
brochure *n.* 宣传册
catalog *n.* 目录
literature *n.* 文字说明

(*After visiting Ford's factory, Jorge is requesting some printed materials concerning the products he is interested in.*)

Jorge: It was very kind of you to show me round the place. It gave me a good idea of your product range.
Ford: It's a pleasure to show our factory to our customers. What's your general impression, may I ask?
Jorge: Very impressive, indeed, especially the speed of your NW Model.
Ford: That's our latest development[1]. It's a product with high performance. We launched it just two months ago.

Jorge: The machine gives you an edge over your competitors, I guess[2].
Ford: Certainly. No one can match us as far as speed is concerned[3].
Jorge: Could you give me some brochures for that machine? And the price if possible.
Ford: Right. Here is our sales catalog and literature.
Jorge: Thank you. I think we may be able to work together in the future.

 Notes:

1. That's our latest development. 那是我们最新开发的产品。
2. The machine gives you an edge over your competitors, I guess. 我想这机器让你们走在对手前面了。
3. No one can match us as far as speed is concerned. 就速度而言,还没有哪一家公司能和我们比。

Questions:
1. How does Jorge feel about Ford's factory?
2. What seems to be very impressive to Jorge?
3. What does Ford tell Jorge about the NW Model.
4. What was Jorge's request?
5. What does Ford give Jorge?
6. Why do you think Jorge is interested in the product?

Conversation 22

Words and Expressions
sightseeing   *n.* 观光
meet clients   会见客户
all in all   总之
reimburse   *n.* 报销
business expenses   出差费,差旅费
receipt   *n.* 收据
pick up   取

(Kenny finished the business trip in New York, now he's making requests to Anne about the travel charges.)

Anne: Hey Ken, how was your trip to New York?
Kenny: Great, I was able to do some sightseeing as well as meet the new clients.
Anne: So all in all it was a very successful trip?
Kenny: Yep. The real reason I came to see you was to see if you could help me get reimbursed for my business expenses[1].
Anne: No worries. How much do you need to be reimbursed? It's also company policy to check all receipts before we can pay you.
Kenny: No problems. I've got them all right here.
Anne: I'll need you to complete this form, including all expenses.
Kenny: When will I be able to pick up the money[2]?
Anne: If you come back after lunch, I should be able to give it to you.
Kenny: Great. I'll see you then. Bye.

Notes:

1. help me get reimbursed for my business expenses：帮我报销差旅费用。
2. When will I be able to pick up the money? 我什么时候可以来取钱？

Questions:

1. How was Kenny's trip to New York? Did he enjoy it?
2. Why does Kenny come to see Anne?
3. What is the company policy concerning reimbursement?
4. Does Kenny bring all receipts with himself?
5. What does the reimbursement form include?
6. When can Kenny get the money?

Conversation 23

Words and Expressions
higher authorities 上级
marketing campaign 营销活动
so far 到目前为止
proceed v. 继续进行
target market 目标市场
forms of media 媒体形式
aim at 以……为目标

> age group   年龄段
> definitely   *ad.* 肯定地
> briefing   *n.* 简要介绍

(*Jane and Nick are discussing the marketing methods as well as the requirements of the higher authorities.*)

Jane: How have the preparations for the new marketing campaign been going?
Nick: Good so far[1], but we still need to make a few decisions before we can proceed any further.
Jane: What about?
Nick: Who is our target market, what forms of media to use in the campaign as well as the budget.
Jane: Well, I already know that management[2] says we are aiming at the 18 - 25 year old age group and they definitely want to use television advertisements.
Nick: But what about the budget? Television advertisements are the most expensive.
Jane: Leave that to management to decide.
Nick: So what should I tell the staff in my department?
Jane: Have the people in your department prepare some ideas for a television and magazine based media marketing campaign[3].
Nick: OK. We should be able to give you a briefing on what ideas we have come up with in a few days[4].

 **Notes:**

1. good so far：到目前为止还不错。
2. management：管理层。
3. prepare some ideas for a television and magazine based media marketing campaign：准备一些在电视和杂志上登广告的想法。
4. We should be able to give you a briefing on what ideas we have come up with in a few days. 过几天我们会给你一份关于我们想法的简要介绍。

Questions:
1. How are the preparations for the new marketing campaign going so far?
2. What decisions does Nick think they should make?
3. What age group will the campaign aim at?
4. What form of media does management intend to use?
5. What is the work that Jane wants people in Nick's department to do?

6. How does Nick respond to Jane's request?

Conversation 24

Words and Expressions
installments   *n.* 分期付款
prior to   在……之前
delivery   *n.* 交货
first order   初次订购
money trouble   财务困难
make a profit   盈利
consult   *v.* 与……商量
boss   *n.* 老板

(*Sam is explaining to Jane why he requests installment.*)

Jane: If it's OK with you, we would like payment prior to delivery, since this is your first order.
Sam: I understand why you would like it that way[1], but we prefer payment after delivery because these goods are very expensive.
Jane: I know they are very expensive, but why does that mean you should pay after delivery?
Sam: It's a large order, and if we pay in advance, we will run into money trouble[2], because it will take three or four months to sell the goods and start to make a profit.
Jane: I understand, but if we must pay to make the goods, and then must wait four months for you to pay, we will have money trouble, too[3].
Sam: Let's do it this way. We will pay in installments, with the first payment to be two weeks after delivery, then once a month after that.
Jane: It sounds reasonable, but I'll have to consult my boss[4].

 Notes:

1. I understand why you would like it that way. 我知道你们这样做的原因。
2. run into money trouble：发生财务困难。
3. But if we must pay to make the goods … money trouble too. 但如果我们要先花钱生产产品，然后又要等4个月才能拿到货款，我们也会发生财务困难。
4. It sounds reasonable, but I'll have to consult my boss. 听上去很合理，但我得和老板

商量。

Questions:
1. For what reason does Jane want Sam to pay in advance?
2. Why does Sam prefer payment after delivery?
3. What further reason does Sam give for payment after delivery?
4. Does Jane agree with Sam? Why?
5. What does Sam suggest as a new way of payment?
6. How does Jane respond to Sam's suggestion?

Key Expressions

I. Making a request
1. Could/Can/Would you please ...?
2. Do/Would you mind ...?
3. Do you think you could ...?
4. I was wondering if you could ...
5. I'd like sb. to ...
6. I'd appreciate it if you could ...
7. I would be grateful if you could ...
8. Could you please send me ...
9. Could you possibly tell us/let us have ...
10. In addition, I would like to receive ...
11. It would be helpful if you could send us ...
12. I am interested in (obtaining/receiving ...)
13. I would appreciate your immediate attention to this matter.
14. Please let me know what action you propose to take.

II. Responding to a request
1. OK./All right./Sure./Certainly./No problem./I'd love to./No, I don't mind at all.
2. No, I'm afraid I can't help you.
3. I'd like to, but ...

III. Asking for permission
1. May/Could/Can I ...?
2. I'm/was wondering if ...?
3. Would/Do you mind ...?
4. Is it all right to ...?

IV. Giving or refusing to give permission
1. Yes, please./Of course./Sure./Certainly./No problem./No, not at all.
2. No, I'm afraid not.
3. Sorry, you can't.
4. No, I'd rather you didn't ...

Workshop

I. Business vocabulary.

1. Give the English for the following business expressions.
   - (1) 销售代表 _____
   - (2) 职位空缺 _____
   - (3) 承担 _____
   - (4) 转变 _____
   - (5) 稳定的需求 _____
   - (6) 试订购 _____
   - (7) 供过于求 _____
   - (8) 高性能 _____
   - (9) 观光 _____
   - (10) 盈利 _____

2. Give the Chinese for the following business expressions.
   - (1) grab one's file _____
   - (2) job advancement _____
   - (3) extra responsibilities _____
   - (4) sound reasonable _____
   - (5) man-made _____
   - (6) business expenses _____
   - (7) forms of media _____
   - (8) target market _____
   - (9) payment prior _____
   - (10) pay in installments _____

3. Complete the sentences by using the words in the box.

merely	delivery	prefer	marketing campaign	installments
pick up	campaign	responsibilities	reduction	prior to

   - (1) I assume there'd be more meetings, paperwork, and other _____, too.
   - (2) I don't mean they are higher _____ by 2 or 3 percent.
   - (3) How can you expect us to make a _____ to that extent?
   - (4) When will I be able to _____ _____ the money?
   - (5) Have the people in your department prepare some ideas for a television and magazine based media _____ _____.
   - (6) I know they are very expensive, but why does that mean you should pay after _____?
   - (7) We will pay in _____, with the first payment to be two weeks after delivery.
   - (8) Who is our target market, what forms of media to use in the _____ as well as the budget?
   - (9) We would like payment _____ _____ delivery, since this is your first order.
   - (10) We _____ payment after delivery, because these goods are very expensive.

II. Complete the following conversations based on the Chinese given.

Conversation 1
Jenny: _____ (我们能讨论一下我的薪水吗)?
Li Yan: Sure.
Jenny: I really like working for this company. Do you think I'm doing a good job here?
Li Yan: _____ (是的,你是名努力的员工).
Jenny: But the problem is, my salary just isn't enough to live on, even for food and rent.
Li Yan: What's your opinion?
Jenny: _____ (我想加薪 5%).
Li Yan: _____ (那可有点多). If I give you a rise, I have to give everyone a rise.
Jenny: Listen, if you pay me more, _____ (我会承担更多的工作).
Li Yan: That sounds reasonable. How about this, from now on, you will be responsible for scheduling. That means _____ (如果你找不到人的话), you'll have to do it.
Jenny: That sounds good to me. I really appreciate it.

Conversation 2
Alice: The size of our trial order depends greatly on the prices. _____ (让我们先解决那个问题吧).
Green: OK, if your order is large enough, we're ready to reduce our prices by 5 percent.
Alice: When I say your prices are much too high, I don't mean they are higher merely by 2 or 3 percent.
Green: How much do you mean then? _____ (你能说一个大概的数字吗)?
Alice: I should say a reduction of least 8 percent would help.
Green: That's impossible. _____ (你怎么能要求我们给那么大的折扣呢)?
Alice: I think you are as well-informed as I am about the market for chemical fertilizers. It's unnecessary for me to point out that supply exceeds demand at present and _____ (这种情况还要持续很长时间). May I suggest that you call your client to confirm that?
Green: OK, I will.

Conversation 3
Mary: If it's OK, _____ (我们希望能在交货前付款) since this is your first order.
Edward: I can understand it, but we prefer payment after delivery because these goods are very expensive.
Mary: I know they are very expensive, _____ (但为什么那意味着要交货后付款呢)?
Edward: If we pay in advance, _____ (我们会发生财务困难), because it will take three or four months to sell the goods and start to make a profit.
Mary: I see, but if we must pay to make the goods, and then must wait four months for you

to pay, we will have money trouble, too.

Edward: Let's do it this way. _____ (我们将分期付款), with the first payment to be two weeks after delivery, then once a month after that.

Mary: It sounds reasonable, but I'll have to consult my boss.

III. Role play.

1. You want to open a bank account at a branch of ICBC bank near your flat. At the service counter, you ask a clerk to tell you the necessary steps of opening a savings account.
2. You have found a new job at a high-tech company in Nanjing, so you and your family are planning to move to Nanjing. Now you ask one of your new colleagues who work at the HR Department to look for an appropriate apartment for you.

Unit 4 Resolving Conflicts

(Conversations 25 – 30)

Don't let conflicts separate you from success! Resolving conflicts in and outside companies is an art. In today's world, being an expert in your field is not always enough. The ability to get along with others, to deal with conflicts, and to make others feel comfortable has become increasingly important. Thus the way we solve conflicts can determine whether we can have a harmonious relationship with colleagues, superiors, and clients etc.. In this unit we are going to learn how to effectively resolve conflicts in the workplace.

Conversation 25

Words and Expressions
hair dryer   吹风机
instruction   *n.* （操作）说明
receipt   *n.* 收据，收条
guarantee   *n.* 保证（书）
guarantee period   保质期
service center   服务中心
collect   *v.* 收集，提取
repair   *v.* 修理

(*Mark is a shop assistant. Lucy is a customer who bought a hair dryer from the shop a few weeks ago and found it didn't work now. Lucy comes to the shop to make complaints to Mark.*)

Mark: Good morning. Can I help you?
Lucy: Yes, I bought this hair dryer in October. Now it doesn't work.
Mark: I see. Have you followed the instructions carefully[1]?
Lucy: Yes. It worked perfectly until last week.
Mark: Do you have the receipt and guarantee[2]?
Lucy: Yes, here you are.
Mark: You're within the guarantee period[3]. We'll send it to the Service Center to be repaired.
Lucy: How long will it take?
Mark: Two weeks. Please come and collect it then. And don't forget to bring the receipt.

Notes:

1. Have you followed the instructions carefully? 你是按照用法说明（操作）吗？
2. Do you have the receipt and guarantee? 你有收据和保单吗？
3. You're within the guarantee period. 你（的产品）还在保修期内。

Questions:

1. Who is Lucy? And who is Mark?
2. What is Lucy complaining about?
3. What does Mark ask Lucy to show her? Why?
4. How does Mark resolve the conflict?

Conversation 26

Words and Expressions
be fed up with 厌倦，厌烦
fire v. 解雇
gossip v. 闲聊，搬弄是非
spread v. 传播，散布
rumor n. 谣言
be down on one's luck 倒霉
negative a. 否定的，消极的
strength n. 强项，长处
weakness n. 弱点，短处
colleague n. 同事

(*Carrie and Victor are coworkers; Carrie is complaining about Helen who gossips and tries to start problems among the employees. Victor tries to solve this conflict.*)

Carrie: I'm really fed up with Helen[1]. Why hasn't the manager fired her yet?
Victor: The management couldn't fire someone just because they gossip.
Carrie: It's not only that she spreads rumors, but she also tries to start problems among the employees[2].
Victor: You will always have such co-workers[3].
Carrie: I am really down on my luck?
Victor: You shouldn't be so negative[4].

Carrie: You can say that because you don't have to work with her.
Victor: Everybody has his strengths and weaknesses[5]. So has Helen.
Carrie: I hope to have a better colleague to work with.

Notes:

1. I'm really fed up with Helen. 我真受够海伦了。
2. It's not only that she spreads rumors, but she also tries to start problems among the employees. 她不仅散布谣言,还试图在员工之间挑起事端。
3. You will always have such co-workers. 你总会碰见这样的同事。
4. You shouldn't be so negative. 你不应该(对她)如此否定。
5. Everybody has his strengths and weaknesses. 每个人都有自己的长处和短处。

Questions:

1. Who are Carrie and Victor talking about?
2. Why does Carrie want the manager to fire Helen?
3. Does Victor agree with Carrie?
4. What is Victor's opinion of Helen?
5. What does Victor suggest to Carrie for resolving the conflict?
6. Do you agree with Victor? Why?

Conversation 27

> **Words and Expressions**
> R&D 研发(＝Research and Development)
> appreciate v. 赏识,觉察
> format   格式
> misread v. 看错,读错
> budget vt. 将(款项)纳入预算,编制预算
> turn up   挖掘而发现
> get back on the horse   重新上马

(*Katharine works in the R&D Department. Jacob is the manager of the department. Jacob talks to Katharine about a mistake she has made.*)

Jacob: Hi Katharine. I want to talk to you about your research work for the website. You did a great job getting a lot of information, and I appreciate the good format you put into the website[1]. There's one problem, though. I think somewhere you must have misread the amount we'd budgeted for designers[2].

Katharine: Oh dear, really?

Jacob: Yes, so it looks almost all the designers you turned up are going to be out of our range[3].

Katharine: I can't believe I did that! I'm so sorry.

Jacob: It's OK, just please be more careful in the future[4]. This research will be relatively easy to redo, but on other projects it might not be.

Katharine: I understand. It won't happen again.

Jacob: I'm sure it won't. Don't worry about it too much; we all make mistakes. Just remember, always check dates, amounts, and numbers first. They're the most important things to get right!

Katharine: I'll remember. Now, I guess I should get back to work on this research.

Jacob: That's right — get back on the horse!

Notes:

1. I appreciate the good format you put into the website. 我很欣赏你在网站中使用这么好的格式。
2. You must have misread the amount we'd budgeted for designers. 你一定是把我们做的设计师预算弄错了。
3. So it looks almost all the designers you turned up are going to be out of our range. 这样你找的设计师几乎都超过我们的预算范围。
4. It's OK, just please be more careful in the future. 没关系，以后更仔细点就行了。

Questions:

1. Who is Jacob? Why does he talk to Katherine?
2. What mistake did Katherine make?
3. How does Katharine feel about the mistake she made?
4. What is Jacob's suggestion to Katharine concerning research work?
5. Do you think Jacob is a good manager?

Conversation 28

Words and Expressions
work overtime　加班
overtime pay　加班工资

> keep one's promise   履行承诺
> influence   n. 影响
> recession   n. 衰退
> global economic recession   全球经济衰退
> depression   n. 不景气,萧条
> considerate   a. 体贴的,关心的
> take something seriously   认真对待

(*Henry is Ella's manager. Ella worked overtime several days ago, but she hasn't got overtime pay yet. Now she is talking with Henry about it.*)

Ella: Manager, you promised to pay overtime, but we still haven't got it.
Henry: Due to the influence of global economic recession and productive depression of our co-company, our products don't sell well[1].
Ella: It has nothing to do with us[2]. You should keep your promise.
Henry: I know it is not reasonable to work overtime without extra pay, but ...
Ella: In fact, my salary has remained the same for two years, even when our company was operating well.
Henry: But it's not proper to complain to the president at this time.
Ella: I don't want to be so considerate. If you don't take it seriously, I shall resign[3].
Henry: Please take your time[4]. Maybe things will change for the better[5].
Ella: I look forward to a reply as soon as possible.

 **Notes:**

1. Due to the influence of global economic recession and productive depression of our co-company, our products don't sell well. 由于受全球经济衰退的影响,加之与我们合作的公司不景气,我们公司产品销路不好。
2. It has nothing to do with us. 这和我们没关系。
3. I don't want to be so considerate. If you don't take it seriously, I shall resign. 我可不管这么多。如果你们不当回事,我就辞职走人。
4. Please take your time. 请不要着急。
5. Maybe things will change for the better. 也许事情会好起来。

Questions:
1. Who are talking in this conversation? Are they friends?
2. What is Ella complaining about?
3. How does Henry respond to Ella's complaint?

4. Does Ella accept the reasons that Henry gives for not paying overtime?
5. What will Ella do if the company does not take matter seriously?
6. What do you think of Henry as a manager?

Conversation 29

Words and Expressions
give sb. a rise/raise 给某人涨工资
financial crisis 金融危机
lose money 亏损
tighten one's belt 勒紧腰带（过日子）
struggle v. 努力,奋斗
be laid off 被解雇
notice v. 通知

(*Mr. Paul is Jessica's boss. Jessica asks Mr. Paul for pay rise.*)

Jessica: Boss, I would like to discuss something with you.
Mr. Paul: Well.
Jessica: I have been working here for three years, and I really should get a pay rise[1].
Mr. Paul: When was the last time you got a raise?
Jessica: Two years ago.
Mr. Paul: I'll think about it. But as you know, the financial crisis is serious now, and our company keeps losing money and I can't afford to give anyone a raise[2].
Jessica: You mean I have to tighten my belt[3]?
Mr. Paul: Our company is struggling these days, and you are lucky enough not being laid off[4].
Jessica: Since you won't give me a rise, you'd better let me have a little more free time.
Mr. Paul: All right. I will notice the personnel department.

 Notes:

1. I really should get a pay rise. 我真该涨工资了。
2. Our company keeps losing money and I can't afford to give anyone a raise. 公司不断亏损,我没法给员工涨工资。
3. You mean I have to tighten my belt? 你的意思是我得勒紧裤腰带过日子?
4. Our company is struggling these days, and you are lucky enough not being laid off. 这些日

子公司也不好过,你没被裁员就够幸运了。

Questions:
1. What does Jessica ask for?
2. How does Mr. Paul respond to Jessica's request?
3. Why does Mr. Paul say that Jessica is lucky?
4. What is Jessica's second request?
5. How does Mr. Paul respond to Jessica's second request?

Conversation 30

Words and Expressions
express   *n.* 急件,快递公司
delivery   *n.* 递送,投递
depot   *n.* 库房,仓库
place an order   下订单
inconvenience   *n.* 不方便,麻烦
assure   *v.* 保证,确保
draw one's attention   请(某人)注意

(*Mark makes a phone call to Diane who works in Royal Express to talk about the delayed delivery.*)

Mark: Hello, can I speak to Royal Express, please?
Diane: Hello, you're through to Royal Express. How can I help you?
Mark: Well, I phoned two days ago to say that I hadn't received delivery of my order and I'm ringing again to say it still hasn't arrived.
Diane: Can I just take your name, please?
Mark: Yes, it's Mark Anderson.
Diane: Ah! I think there's been a problem with that order, Mr. Anderson.
Mark: What kind of problem?
Diane: Let me check for you. Yes, part of the order didn't arrive here at the depot, so I couldn't send it out until we'd received everything.
Mark: Well, surely that was your duty to sort out the problem[1] without my having to call you back again. I did phone and draw your attention to this a couple of days ago[2]. You know, I placed this order weeks ago. It's just not good enough[3].
Diane: Yeah, I'm sorry about this, Mr. Anderson. I'm sorry for the inconvenience, but I can assure you we'll do everything we can to send it out to you as quickly as possible.

Notes:

1. surely that was your duty to sort out the problem：很显然，解决问题是你们的责任。
2. I did phone and draw your attention to this a couple of days ago. 几天前我还给你们打过电话，要你们注意这批物品。
3. It's just not good enough.（我想）这样不好吧。

Questions:

1. What is the relationship between Mark and Diane?
2. Why does Mark phone Diane? What's the problem with the order?
3. According to Diane, what's the reason for the delayed delivery?
4. How does Diane handle Mark's complaint?
5. Do you think the conflict is effectively resolved?

Key Expressions

I. Avoiding
1. Let's discuss this later.
2. Let's forget it.
3. But it's not proper to complain to ... at this time.
4. Would it be a good idea to ...?
5. It's unfair to distrust someone without any reasons.

II. Accommodating
1. I'm sorry. You're right.
2. Go ahead and do it your way.
3. I can't believe I did that! I'm so sorry.
4. Please take your time. Maybe things will change for the better.
5. I'm sorry for the inconvenience, but I can assure you we'll ...
6. Please excuse the mistake.

III. Competing
1. Of course I'm right.
2. Do it my way.
3. It's your mistake.
4. It has nothing to do with us. You should keep your promise.
5. If you don't take it seriously, I shall ...
6. It's unbelievable!
7. I look forward to a reply as soon as possible.

Workshop

I. Business vocabulary.

1. Give the English version for the following business expressions.
    (1) 操作说明 _____
    (2) 保质期 _____
    (3) 服务中心 _____
    (4) 保证书 _____
    (5) 编制预算 _____
    (6) 全球经济衰退 _____
    (7) 履行诺言 _____
    (8) 金融危机 _____
    (9) 亏损 _____
    (10) 投递,交付 _____

2. Give the Chinese version for the following.
    (1) depression _____
    (2) place an order _____
    (3) dispatch _____
    (4) inconvenience _____
    (5) depot _____
    (6) assure _____
    (7) give somebody a raise _____
    (8) receipt _____
    (9) repair _____
    (10) misread _____

3. Complete the sentences by using the words in the box.

negative	*have* complained	*assure*	*laid off*	*appreciate*
drew your attention	*reasonable*	*inconvenience*	*guarantee*	*due to*

    (1) If you give a _____ answer, we shall cancel the order.
    (2) We certainly _____ your difficulty in spreading the sale of our goods.
    (3) We _____ to our letter dated 31st August, 2012, but your reply is still awaiting.
    (4) We can _____ you of the reliability of the advertising effectiveness.
    (5) The quality is good and the price is _____.
    (6) With less orders coming in, many employees were _____.
    (7) Our users _____ to us about the damage of the goods.
    (8) We do apologize for the great _____ it's going to cause you.
    (9) The air-conditioner is sold with a twelve-month _____.
    (10) The decline of the market is _____ the decrease in demand.

Workplace Communication Skills 工作场所交流技能

II. Complete the dialogues by choosing the sentences from the box.

> A. I can't believe I did that! I'm so sorry.
> B. I think there's been problem with that order.
> C. I'm sorry for this convenience.
> D. All right. I will notice the personnel department.
> E. If you don't take it seriously, I shall resign.

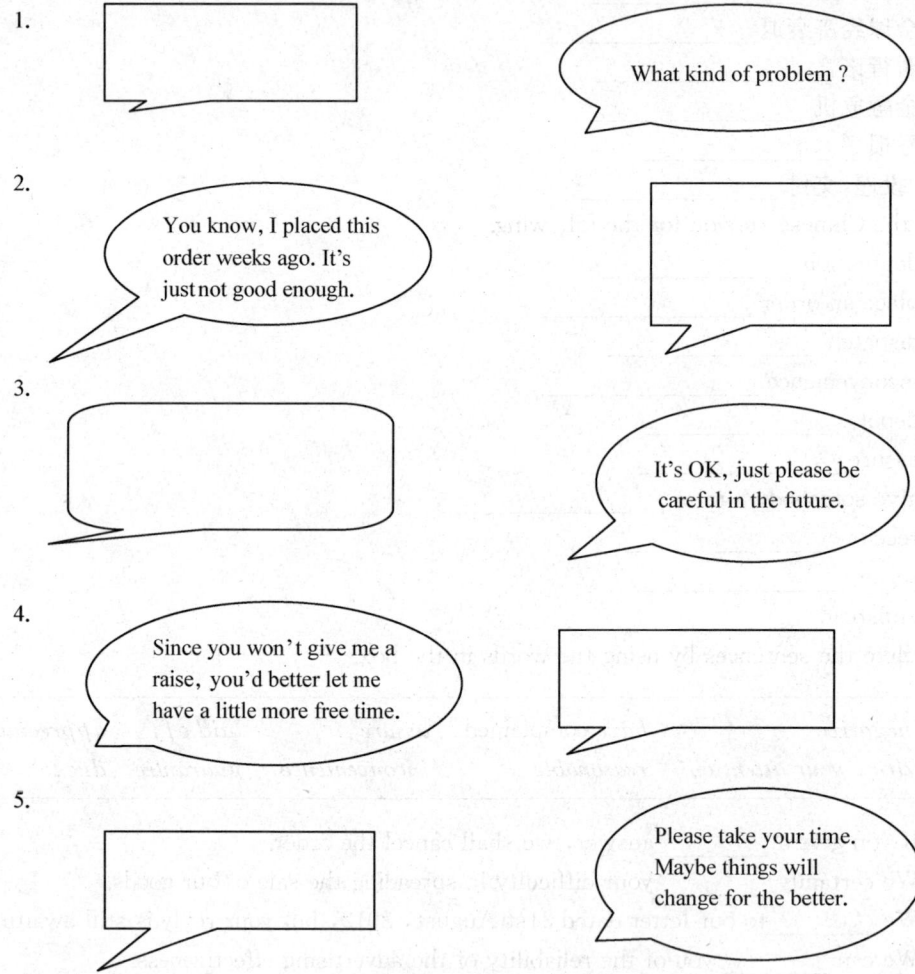

III. Complete the following conversations based on the Chinese given.

Conversation 1

Sara: I'd like to speak to the manager of _____ (服务中心).
Bill: Speaking.
Sara: Last week I bought a Digital camera from your company, but _____ (今天它

不好用了）.
Bill: _____ (抱歉，先生). I'll replace it for you if you may show us your _____ _____ (保证书和发票).
Sara: It's OK. See you.

Conversation 2
Sheila: I can get along with most of my colleagues except John. He is a pain in the neck!
Den: _____ (你不应该这么否定他).
Sheila: You only say that because you don't have to work with him. He always makes careless mistakes, and always tries to find excuse for not taking the responsibilities.
Den: _____ (你总会碰见这样的同事). But _____ (每个人都有自己的长处和短处). Maybe you should think more about his strong points. John is not no good at all. He works very hard, and never mind _____ (加班).

Conversation 3
Sheila: I have something unpleasant to talk to you about. The goods you send us can't reach us in due time because of the bad weather.
Walt: Really? _____ (真是令人难以置信)
Sheila: Yes, and the shipper informed us that the packing of goods were damaged seriously.
Walt: As far as I know, the goods were in perfect condition when they left here.
Sheila: _____ (请调查一下这件事，并立即予以解决).
Walt: We'll get in touch with the shipping company and see what can be done.
Sheila: _____ (我希望尽快有一个答复).

IV. Group work.
A customer is complaining to a hotel clerk. Put the sentences in order. Then try to role play it.
1. I'm sorry about that. Would you like me to put you in another room?
2. Please excuse the mistake. I'll send up a newspaper immediately. Would that be acceptable?
3. What's the problem?
4. I apologize for the delay. Quite a few of our staff are ill today so things are taking a bit longer. I'll arrange somebody to take care of it right away.
5. I asked for a non-smoking room, but my room smells of smoke.
6. OK, that'll be fine. I have one last problem. I wanted a newspaper delivered to my room, but I didn't get one this morning.
7. Good morning. I need your help. There's a mistake with my hotel room.
8. Yes, please. There's another thing. I asked somebody to pick up my dirty laundry two hours ago but nobody has shown up.
9. Yes, thank you for your help.

V. Role play.
1. Suppose you talk with your boss about the promotion which you deserved a year ago.

2. Your client complains about the faulty goods. You offer a solution to the problem and tell him what you will do.
3. Your co-worker uploads your essay on the internet without your consent. You deal with this problem and request him to apologize to you.

Unit 5 Exchanging Ideas

(Conversations 31 – 35)

Workplace communication involves a lot of exchanges of ideas. It is true that the basic or routine tasks in any workplace consist of gathering and conveying information, giving and receiving instructions, however, these types of communication are not enough. Very often, people have to talk about something in depth. A good exchange of ideas may bring forth new ideas that will work better. Therefore, a good communicator should know how to exchange ideas with his/her co-workers, superiors, clients, etc.. In this unit we are going to learn how to use communication skills to exchange ideas politely and effectively in the workplace.

Conversation 31

> **Words and Expressions**
> sales figure   销售数字,销售额
> market share   市场份额
> brand   *n.* 品牌
> cut down on cost   降低成本
> advertising expense   广告费用
> worthwhile   *a.* 值得的
> in that case   那样的话

(*Alan and Jill are co-workers. They meet in the office and exchange ideas about the sales figures last year.*)
Alan: Jack, here are the sales figures of our products last year.

Jill: How is that?

Alan: Good, but I think it could be better[1].

Jill: How? Have you got any idea on your mind?

Alan: I believe if we build our own brand, we can definitely sell more[2].

Jill: That's exactly the way I feel.

Alan: In that case, we can set higher prices for our products and have a bigger market share, which will surely lead to more profits[3].

Jill: Exactly!

(... *They shift their talk to advertising expenses.*)

Alan: It might be that we should[4] cut down on costs by reducing the advertising expenses.

Jill: I have a slightly different view on that.

Alan: What's your point of view?

Jill: I think advertising expenses are worthwhile, but I don't think radio advertising is useful to our products.

Alan: It seems we agree on cutting advertising expenses, but we need to further discuss which part of advertising we should cut to save costs.

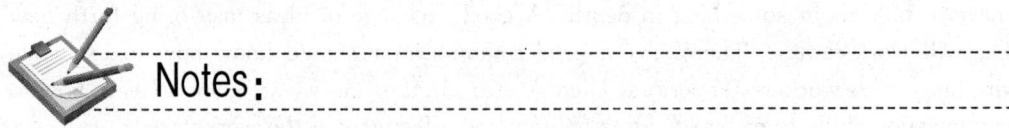

1. Good, but I think it could be better. 不错，但我觉得可以更好。
2. I believe if we build our own brand, we can definitely sell more. 我认为如果我们创建自己的品牌，一定能销得更多。
3. In that case, we can set higher prices for our products and have a bigger market share, which will surely lead to more profits. 那样的话，我们就能提高产品价格，获取更大的市场份额，从而带来更丰厚的利润。
4. It might be that we should ... 也许我们应该……

Questions:
1. Who are talking in this conversation? Are they friends?
2. What are Alan and Jill talking about?
3. What does Alan think of the sales figures?
4. What does Alan suggest to further increase the sales?
5. Does Jill agree with Alan?
6. What's Alan's view about the company's advertising expenses?
7. Does Jill fully agree with Alan?
8. What's Jill's view about the advertising expenses?

Conversation 32

Words and Expressions

come up with　想出
brainstorming　*n.* 头脑风暴
time-management　时间管理
suggest　*v.* 建议
understaffed　*a.* 人员不足,人手不足
impact　*n.* 影响
output　*n.* 产量
workload　*n.* 工作量
it is time to　到……的时候了,该做……了
lighten　*v.* 减轻
load　*n.* 负担,负荷

(*Carrie and Victor are coworkers; they meet to discuss ideas about the time-management for the office.*)

Carrie: We've got to come up with a way to solve this problem[1]! No one is getting all their work done during the work day. We need to do some brainstorming to come up with a time-management solution for our office.

Victor: Well, what do you suggest? It's not that we are all wasting a lot of time[2]. Fact is, we're understaffed. People just have too much to do.

Carrie: So you think we should hire some new people? That is one possible solution. What else could be the problem?

Victor: Maybe we do have some problems with time-management. If people were always on time to work, they might get more done in the morning before lunch.

Carrie: That's true. Also, maybe we could shorten the lunch break from an hour to 45 minutes. That would add a little time to everyone's day.

Victor: Fifteen minutes would be good, but I wonder if it would make a big impact on the employees' output[3]. I still think it's a problem with too much workload.

Carrie: We ended up right where we started[4]. Maybe it is time to look for some temp workers to help with a few projects[5]. That would lighten everyone's load.

Notes:

1. We've got to come up with a way to solve this problem! 我们得想个办法来解决这个问题!
2. It's not that we are all wasting a lot of time. 并不是我们都在浪费了大量时间。
3. Fifteen minutes would be good, but I wonder if it would make a big impact on the employees' output. 午餐缩短15分钟也许有用,但会不会对员工的业绩产生大的影响却未必。
4. We ended up right where we started. 我们最终又回到了开始时的话题。
5. Maybe it is time to look for some temp workers to help with a few projects. 也许该是找一些临时的员工来帮帮忙的时候了。

Questions:

1. Who are talking in this conversation? Are they friends?
2. What are Carrie and Victor talking about?
3. What is the problem Carrie wants to discuss with Victor?
4. What does Carrie suggest to solve the problem in the office?
5. According to Victor, what is the reason for the problem?
6. What is the possible solution according to Carrie?
7. What is the possible solution according to Victor?
8. What does Carrie suggest to lighten the workload?

Conversation 33

Words and Expressions
get out of　摆脱
asset　*n.* 资产
equipment　*n.* 设备
cash　*n.* 现金
make sense　有道理
run a business　经营企业
coffee brewer　咖啡机

(*Sarah is one of Phil's clients. She turns to Phil for business advice. They discuss the ways to get Sarah out of the difficult situation.*)

Sarah: I'm really in a difficult situation here. I don't know if I'm going to be able to get out of this successfully. What should I do, Phil?

Phil: Well, I've really never been in that kind of situation before. But if it were me, I would start by selling some of my assets[1]. You could sell some of your equipment.

Sarah: Why's that?

Phil: Well, then you would have more cash.

Sarah: I guess that makes sense. But I just don't know that I can run my business without all of that equipment. Who runs a coffee shop without a coffee brewer[2]?

Phil: I'm not trying to tell you how to run your business, just what I would do if I were in your place[3].

Sarah: And you just might be right[4]. Thank you for your advice.

Notes:

1. But if it were me, I would start by selling some of my assets. 要是换成我,我会先卖出一部分资产。
2. Who runs a coffee shop without a coffee brewer? 谁经营咖啡店而又没有咖啡机呢?(言下之意是离开了那些设备就无法经营了。)
3. I'm not trying to tell you how to run your business, just what I would do if I were in your place. 我不是在教你如何经营企业,我只是告诉你,如果我处在你的位置,我会怎么做。
4. And you just might be right. 你也许是对的。

Questions:

1. Why does Sarah ask Phil for business advice?
2. What does Phil suggest Sarah to do?
3. What reason does Phil give for his suggestion?
4. Is Sarah ready to take Phil's advice? Why?

Conversation 34

Words and Expressions
partnership   *n.* 合伙(企业)
education   *n.* 教育
educational   *a.* 教育的
anything but   决不会,绝对不会
unbiased   *a.* 没有偏见的
independent organization   独立机构
trick into   诱骗

> skeptical *a.* 怀疑的
> informed decision 知情的决定
> board *n.* 董事会

(*Carl is one of Ella's clients. They are talking about forming a business partnership.*)

Ella: I feel that getting into the education market could really increase your sales. That's why I want you to consider joining us on this project.

Carl: I don't know about that[1]. But in my opinion, we're an entertainment company. We don't want to turn away our clients with boring educational materials[2].

Ella: With our help, I believe they'll be anything but boring. I would like to add that we have plans for videotaped classes that have tested well in our target audiences[3].

Carl: How well? Are you sure these tests were unbiased and accurate?

Ella: Quite sure. We had them done by an independent organization. We're not trying to trick you into anything, Carl.

Carl: Oh, I wasn't trying to say that[4]. It's just my job to be skeptical, you know.

Ella: Let me tell you all the figures and then you can make an informed decision.

Carl: As far as I'm concerned these figures do look promising. But we need the approval of the board before we can do that.

Notes:

1. I don't know about that. 这个我不清楚。
2. We don't want to turn away our clients with boring educational materials. 我们可不想让这些乏味的教育资料将我们的客户拒之门外。
3. I would like to add that we have plans for videotaped classes that have tested well in our target audiences. 我想补充的是,我们计划推出录像课程,这些课程在目标观众中试用时效果很好。
4. Oh, I wasn't trying to say that. 哦,我并无此意。

Questions:

1. Who is Ella? Who is Carl? Are they friends?
2. What are Ella and Carl discussing?
3. What does Ella want Carl to do?
4. Is Carl interested in Ella's proposal? Why?
5. Why does Ella mention the video classes?
6. Does Carl believe in what Ella tells him?
7. Is Carl able to make a decision? Why?

Conversation 35

Words and Expressions
on schedule　按时
complete　*a.* 完整的, 全部的
advice　*n.* 建议
approve　*v.* 批准, 赞成
information system　信息系统
reduce　*v.* 减少
communication error　信息错误
effective　*a.* 有效的
efficient　*a.* 有效率的

(*Rita and Den are coworkers. Rita wants to have Den's advise on her project.*)

Rita: I have finished my project on schedule. Would you have a look at it and advise me if there's anything[1]?

Den: Um-hmm. In general, I believe you've provided sound and complete information in the report. But in my opinion, we still need to improve the information system, for it is our weakest link[2].

Rita: So do you have any advice on that?

Den: If we improve the information system, we will be able to reduce communication errors. And the communication will be more effective and efficient.

Rita: Good point. This is the way we can go for it[3]. We should get the project approved this time if we improve the information system.

Notes:

1. Would you like to review it and advise me if there's anything? 请你看看, 能否给我提点建议?
2. our weakest link: 我们最薄弱的环节。
3. This is the way we can go for it. 这是我们可以做的事。

Questions:
1. About what does Rita want to talk to Den?
2. What does Rita want Den to do?
3. What advice does Den give?

4. Does Rita agree with Den?

Key Expressions

I. Asking for opinions
1. Would you please . . . ?
2. Any advice on that?
3. What do/would you suggest?
4. What is your point/opinion?
5. Do you have any suggestion?
6. Any comment?

II. Giving opinions
1. I think/feel/believe . . .
2. In my opinion . . .
3. As far as I'm concerned . . .
4. I would like to add that . . .
5. What I'm trying to say is . . .
6. But if it were me, I would . . .

III. Showing agreement
1. That's exactly the way I feel.
2. I agree with what you said.
3. I totally agree with you.
4. I can't agree with you more.
5. I'm in favor of your idea.
6. I have no better idea than this so far.

IV. Showing disagreement
1. That's not how I see it.
2. I have a slightly different view on that.
3. I'm afraid I can't agree. I'm afraid I'm not convinced.
4. I don't agree with you.
5. I don't think that's the case.
6. I think your argument just doesn't hold up.
7. I'm sorry, but I can't accept your point of view.

Workshop

I. Business vocabulary.

1. Give the English version for the following business expressions.

(1) 产量 _____

(2) 资产 _____

(3) 品牌 _____

(4) 现金 _____

(5) 信息系统 ＿＿＿＿＿＿
　　(6) 时间管理 ＿＿＿＿＿＿
　　(7) 集体讨论 ＿＿＿＿＿＿
　　(8) 市场份额 ＿＿＿＿＿＿
　　(9) 人员不足 ＿＿＿＿＿＿
　　(10) 广告费用 ＿＿＿＿＿＿
2. Give the Chinese version for the following.
　　(1) workload ＿＿＿＿＿＿
　　(2) impact ＿＿＿＿＿＿
　　(3) up-market ＿＿＿＿＿＿
　　(4) lighten everyone's load ＿＿＿＿＿＿
　　(5) come up with ＿＿＿＿＿＿
　　(6) get out of ＿＿＿＿＿＿
　　(7) independent organization ＿＿＿＿＿＿
　　(8) informed decision ＿＿＿＿＿＿
　　(9) cut down on cost ＿＿＿＿＿＿
　　(10) equipment ＿＿＿＿＿＿
3. Complete the sentences by using the words in the box.

| brainstorming | output | in that case | anything but | trick into | worthwhile |
| understaffed | efficient | come up with | market share | impact | |

　　(1) He is an ＿＿＿＿ student.
　　(2) The scientist ＿＿＿＿ an effective method.
　　(3) The office is ＿＿＿＿ since the last secretary left.
　　(4) The car factory hopes to increase its ＿＿＿＿ by 30% next year.
　　(5) The computer has made a great ＿＿＿＿ on modern life.
　　(6) He lives in a large house. He is ＿＿＿＿ poor.
　　(7) She ＿＿＿＿ me ＿＿＿＿ admitting responsibility.
　　(8) We queued for ages, but it was ＿＿＿＿. The concert was fantastic.
　　(9) "I'm afraid I can't give you a discount of 5%..." "Well, ＿＿＿＿ we have to leave the business as it is."
　　(10) The company leads in the production of cars. It occupies the largest ＿＿＿＿ in China.

II. Complete the dialogues by choosing the sentences from the box.

> A. Would you like to review it and advise me?
> B. And you just might be right. Thank you for you advice.
> C. I suggest we build our own brand of products.
> D. Well, what do you suggest?
> E. Then what's your point of view?

Workplace Communication Skills 工作场所交流技能

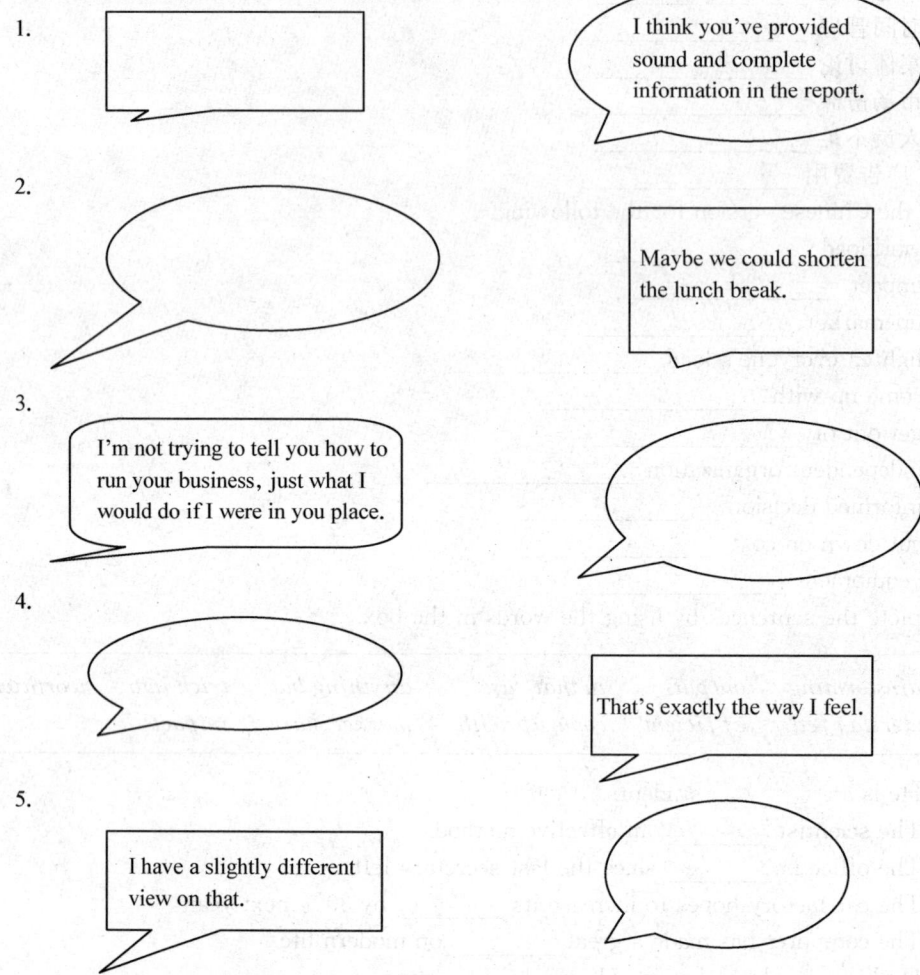

1. [blank]
   — I think you've provided sound and complete information in the report.

2. [blank]
   — Maybe we could shorten the lunch break.

3. I'm not trying to tell you how to run your business, just what I would do if I were in you place.
   — [blank]

4. [blank]
   — That's exactly the way I feel.

5. I have a slightly different view on that.
   — [blank]

III. Complete the following conversations based on the Chinese given.

Conversation 1

A: It seems that the sales figures of our products after the launching have not been quite satisfactory. What shall we do?

B: I don't think the R&D department made enough market research.

C: _____ (我不能同意你的看法).

B: How do you see it then?

C: It's just that sales promotion isn't being well-done.

B: I'm afraid _____ (不能对你的话信服).

Conversation 2

Sarah: _____ (我认为) we can double our profits by supplying a wider variety of office products. I think we've lost too many clients because we only supply paper.

Bill: That's all well and good, but how can we expand in such a competitive market?

Sarah: _____ (如果你问我的话,我觉得) we should firstly make a detailed marketing strategy. Maybe, we can meet with the other department managers someday to talk about it.

Bill: That's a good idea. I'll get in touch with everyone later today.

Sarah: Thanks. _____ (对开拓新的市场,你个人有什么建议)?

Bill: _____ (就我而言), we can expand our product line by partnering with the local suppliers.

Conversation 3

Sheila: So, let's move on to the topic of release date. Gentlemen, when do you think we will be able to launch this product? _____ (大家有什么意见吗)? ... Walt?

Walt: Well, I tend to feel that ... we should probably be able to start testing the product in April. That means that if all goes well, we can have a first release in May or June.

Sheila: I see. Thank you, Walt. _____ (你的观点如何), Bruce?

Bruce: May or June. ... Well, from my point of view... that sounds about right.

George: Excuse me, may I come in here? I wonder if I could say something?

Sheila: Go ahead, George. _____ (你有什么需要补充的吗)?

George: Well, it seems to me that May is much, much too early. Actually, we still have some problems with bugs (故障) in the update engine, and I just don't see how we will be able to fix them.

IV. Role play.

1. Suppose you talk with your coworker about the possibility of setting up a new business in America. You ask for his/her opinions.
2. Your client wants to expand his business to China. He/she is unfamiliar with Chinese market. He/she turns to you. You are to give your opinions about Chinese market.
3. You exchange ideas about the marketing strategy the company adopts. You may agree or disagree with your coworker's opinion.

Unit 6 Giving and Receiving Instructions

(Conversations 36 – 40)

An instruction is a message describing how something is to be done. We give or receive instructions all the time. If we buy a new appliance, for example, we receive instructions on how to install or use it. If there is a new procedure for a work task, employees need instructions on how to do the task. The purpose of instruction is to help people learn. The key to improving our instruction is to know what methods of instruction to use and when.

Conversation 36

Words and Expressions
press   *v.* 按
button   *n.* 按键
transfer   *v.* 切换
dial   *v.* 拨号
hang up   挂断电话

One-Step Instructions
A: Excuse me. Can you help me for a minute?
B: Sure. What is it?
A: Can you show me how to turn on this machine?
B: Yes. Press this button.
A: I see. Thanks very much.
B: You are welcome.

Two-Step Instructions
A: Excuse me. Could you help me for a minute?
B: Certainly. What is it?
A: Could you tell me how to transfer a call[1]?
B: Sure. Press the red button. Then dial the other office and hang up[2].
A: I see. First, I press the red button. Then, I dial the other office and hang up. Right?
B: Yes. That's right.
A: Thank you.

B: You are welcome.

Notes:

1. transfer a call：切换电话。
2. Then dial the other office and hang up. 再拨那个办公室的电话号码，然后挂掉。

Questions:
1. What does A want to do?
2. What is the last step?

Pair work:
Each makes a list of the electrical or mechanical appliances you are familiar with. Then explain to your partner how you use them and answer your partner's questions.

Conversation 37

Words and Expressions
lock   *v.* 锁
cash register   收银机
tray   *n.* 托盘
drawer   *n.* 抽屉

A: How's your first day on the job going[1]?
B: Fine.
A: Tell me, do you know how to lock the cash register[2]?
B: No, I don't. Could you possibly show me how?
A: All right. First, take out your tray. Then, close the drawer[3].
B: I'm sorry. Could you please repeat that?
A: Sure. First, take out your tray.
B: Um-hmm.
A: Then, close the drawer. Okay so far?
B: Yes. I'm following you.
A: Then, turn the key this way[4]. Have you got that?
B: Yes. I understand.

Workplace Communication Skills 工作场所交流技能

A: Be sure to ask if you have any questions.
B: Okay. Thank you very much.

Notes:

1. How's your first day on the job going? 你第一天的工作怎么样啊?
2. lock the cash register: 锁收银机。
3. First, take out your tray. Then, close the drawer. 先拿出托盘,然后关上抽屉。
4. Then, turn the key this way. 朝这个方向转动钥匙。

Questions:

1. How does B feel about his/her first day on the job?
2. Does B know how to lock the cash register?
3. What is A showing B to do?
4. What does B want A to repeat?

Play a game:

Guessing Game: What am I describing?
Using this model, give three instructions for how to do something. Have others guess what you're describing.

Conversation 38

Words and Expressions
confused　*a.* 被弄糊涂的
colleague　*n.* 同事
send a message　发邮件
menu　*n.* 菜单
scroll down　向下滚动,拉下

(*Paulo is confused. He is asking Mari, his colleague, for help.*)
Paulo: Hi, Mari. Thanks for coming. I'm having some trouble with this new email system. Could you give me a hand[1]?

Mari: Sure, what are you trying to do?
Paulo: I'm trying to send a message but I don't know how to send it.
Mari: All right, let's have a look then.
Paulo: Thanks. I just can't get it to go[2].
Mari: Right. This is where you type the subject of the message[3].
Paulo: Uh huh. I did that.
Mari: And this is where you write the email address.
Paulo: OK. I see. Here's the address.
Mari: Yeah. And then go to the "file" menu. OK?
Paulo: OK.
Mari: Then you just scroll down to "send" and then click "send"[4].
Paulo: Uh huh.
Mari: And remember to wait till you see the message has been sent.
Paulo: Got it. Thanks. Mari. Can I get you a coffee?
Mari: Thanks — that would be great.

Notes:

1. Could you give me a hand? 你能帮个忙吗？
2. I just can't get it to go. 我就是发不出去。
3. type the subject of the message：输入你所写邮件的主题。
4. scroll down to "send" and then click "send"：滚动到"send"位置，然后点击"send"。

Questions:

1. Why is Paulo confused? What help does he want?
2. What is Paulo trying to do?
3. Are email messages difficult to send? Can you explain how to send an email message?
4. What does Paulo offer Mari for her help?

Conversation 39

Words and Expressions
Accounts/Purchasing Department   财务/采购部
shredder   *n.* 碎纸机
operating instructions   操作指南
stuff   *n.* 东西
jam   *v.* 卡(纸)

Workplace Communication Skills 工作场所交流技能

> insert   *v.* 插入
> remove   *v.* 移动
> excess   *a.* 过量的
> overheat   *v.* 过热
> switch off   关掉
> automatically   *adv.* 自动地

(*The Accounts Department has bought a new shredder. The secretary, Amy, has a problem. She calls Bob in the Purchasing Department.*)

Bob: Purchasing Department.
Amy: Hi Bob. It's Amy from Accounts here.
Bob: Hi.
Amy: Bob, some questions about the new shredder we've just bought. Everyone keeps asking how to use it and I can't find the operating instructions.
Bob: Ah! Now I think they may still be here. Hold on a second... Yes, I've got them here, Amy. What do you want to know?
Amy: Well, what to do if it doesn't work, you know, stuff like that[1].
Bob: Well. It says here that the machine jams if you insert too much paper into it[2], and if that happens, press the red button, remove the excess paper and start again with less paper.
Amy: Right. Are there any other possible problems?
Bob: The motor overheats sometimes. If that happens, it switches off automatically[3]. Just leave it for 15 to 30 minutes before you switch it on again.
Amy: OK, I've got all that. Is there anything else I should know?
Bob: Yes, there are a few things to be careful about — like never put your fingers in the shredder.
Amy: That's a bit obvious, isn't it?
Bob: And be careful with long hair and loose articles of clothing like ties. And that's it.
Amy: Thanks, Bob. I'll put a notice with the instructions on the wall next to the shredder.
Bob: Good idea.

 **Notes:**

1. what to do if it doesn't work, you know, stuff like that: 机器不正常时该如何操作,以及诸如此类的问题。
2. the machine jams if you insert too much paper into it: 如果你纸插太多,机器会卡住。
3. it switches off automatically: 它会自动关掉。

Questions:
1. What problem does Amy have?
2. What will usually cause the machine to jam?
3. What should people do if the machine jams?
4. What will happen if the motor overheats? When will it start again?
5. What should people be careful about when using the shredder?
6. What will Amy do after the call?

Exercise:
1. What is Amy's problem?
2. Complete Amy's notice.

Instructions for use of shredder
What to do:
Cautions!

Conversation 40

Words and Expressions
memo   n. 备忘录
staff   n. （全体）员工
preferred   a. 选择的,偏爱的
responsive   a. 响应的
represent   v. 代表
permission   n. 允许
applicable   a. 合适的,需要的
recipient   n. 接受者,受话人

(*John, the HR manager of ABC company, is giving instruction on how to answer the phone well at work to his secretary, Amy.*)

John: Amy, could you write a memo to all staff today?

Amy: Sure. What is it about?

John: About how to answer the phone well at work.

Amy: OK. I am taking notes.

John: First, speak clearly. Use the company's preferred greeting[1], like: "Good morning, ABC company, what can I do for you?"

Amy: OK. Speak clearly. Use the company's preferred greeting.

John: Second, be polite and responsive, giving the caller your full attention[2]. Remember that at that moment, you represent the company.

Amy: Uh huh. I've got it.

John: Third, be as helpful as possible, even if it's not exactly your job to answer the phone.

Amy: Third, be as helpful as ... OK, next?

John: Next, ask permission first if you must put the caller on hold: "Would you mind holding for 1 minute?"

Amy: I'm sorry, I didn't catch that. Would you ...?

John: Would you mind holding for 1 minute.

Amy: Got it. This is the fourth.

John: Fifth, take a good message if applicable and pass it on to the recipient[3].

Amy: Yes.

John: The last but not the least, thank the caller.

Amy: OK! I've written down all these. I will finish this memo this morning.

John: Remember to send it to me before you send it to all staff.

Amy: Got it.

John: Thanks.

Notes:

1. Use the company's preferred greeting：使用公司选择的招呼语。
2. giving the caller your full attention：注意力要集中在发话人身上。
3. take a good message if applicable and pass it on to the recipient：如需要，做好记录并转交给受话人。

Questions:

1. What does John instruct Amy to do?
2. What is Amy doing while John is giving instructions?
3. How many steps does John mention?
4. What is the company's preferred greeting?
5. What does John mention as the "last but not the least" thing?
6. When will Amy finish the memo?

Key Expressions

I. Giving instructions
1. First, speak clearly.
2. Second, be polite and responsive.
3. Third, be as helpful as possible.
4. If that happens, press the red button.
5. This is where you write the email address.
6. And then go to the "file" menu.
7. Just leave it for 5 minutes before you switch it on again.
8. Turn the key this way. Got it?

II. Receiving instructions
1. Yes.
2. I see.
3. Yes, I understand.
4. Got it. Thanks.
5. I've got it.
6. I've got all that.
7. OK. I'm taking notes.

III. Asking for clarification
1. I'm sorry, I didn't catch that.
2. Could you repeat that, please?
3. What did you say?
4. Please speak more slowly.
5. What does (... ingredient) mean?
6. I'm sorry, I don't know what you mean.

Workshop

I. Vocabulary.

1. Give the right instructions.
    (1) (Pull/Punch in) this chain.   (Pull)
    (2) (Press/Pull) this lever.   (   )
    (3) (Put in/Press) your time card.   (   )
    (4) (Push/Pull) that button.   (   )
    (5) (Flip/Put in) this switch.   (   )
    (6) (Pull/Press) those buttons.   (   )
    (7) (Punch in/Turn off) the dishwasher.   (   )
    (8) (Turn on/Punch in) this machine.   (   )

2. Help your Co-worker.

    | button   time card   switch   press   chain   pull |

(1) Can you show me how to punch in? Sure. Put in your <u>time card</u>.
(2) Can you show me how to open this? Yes. Push this _____.
(3) Can you show me how to start this? Sure. Flip this _____.
(4) Can you tell me how to turn this off? Sure. _____ this button.
(5) Can you show me how to turn this on? Yes. Pull that _____.
(6) Can you show me how to turn this off? Yes. _____ the chain.

3. Finish the sentence.

   __d__ (1) Transfer   a. the handle
   _____ (2) Lift   b. your hours here
   _____ (3) Sign   c. the phone
   _____ (4) List   d. this call, please
   _____ (5) Hang up   e. your name

4. Giving instructions.

   | sign | set | list | dial | turn on |
   | flip | hang up | put | press | |

   (1) A: Could you tell me how to fill in this timesheet?
       B: Certainly <u>put</u> your employee number here. _____ your hours and _____ your name at the bottom.
   (2) A: Can you please tell me how to transfer a call?
       B: Sure. _____ the red button. Then _____ the other number and _____.
   (3) A: How do you use the postage machine?
       B: First, _____ the amount. Then _____ the envelope in.
   (4) A: How do you I light this oven?
       B: First, _____ a match near the hole. Then _____ the gas.
   (5) A: Could you tell me how to use the ice-cream machine?
       B: Sure. _____ the switch. Then _____ the button to turn the machine on.

5. Work in pairs.
   One student chooses one of the devices and asks the other student what device it is and how to use it.

   | DVD player | computer | digital camera | digital video | projector | fax machine |
   | shredder | printer | copy machine | calculator | cell phone | |

   digital camera

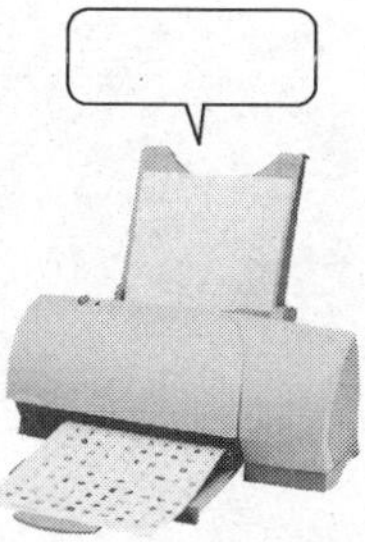

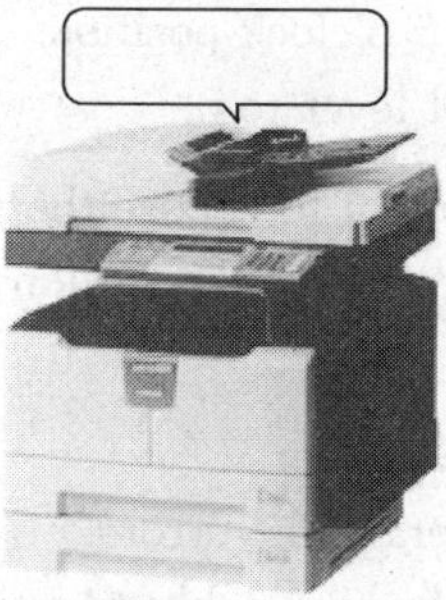

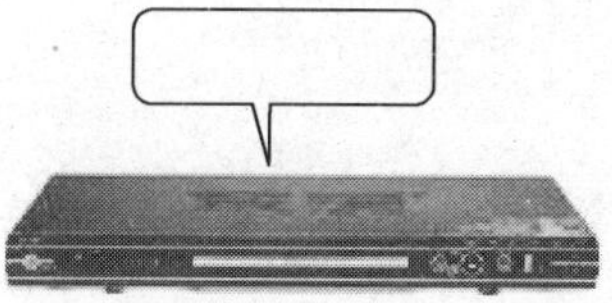

Part 1 Workplace Conversations

6. Put the following verbs into the groups below. You can use some verbs more than once.

| dial | jam | enlarge | reduce | press | print |
| insert | shred | switch on | overheat | send | copy |

Fax machine   **Printer**   **Copy machine**   **Shredder**
dial

II. Listen to each instruction that your teacher reads out to you. As you listen decide the correct order of each of the following. Write in the given spaces, 1, 2, 3 or 4 to indicate their correct order.

1. ☐ Make sure everyone is out of the building.
   ☐ Close all the doors and windows.
   ☐ Call the fire station.

2. ▢ Cover the machine after cleaning.
   ▢ Clean the machine.
   ▢ Switch off and remove the plug from the socket.

3. ▢ Remove the used paper roll.
   ▢ Put in the new roll.
   ▢ Switch off the power and unplug the machine.
   ▢ Pull the paper roll knobs outwards.

4. ▢ Return the pressure control lever to 0.
   ▢ Put the handle in the 6 o'clock position.
   ▢ Return the ink control lever to 0.

5. ▢ Adjust the volume control to choose the right level.
   ▢ Turn the knob to select the radio station you want.
   ▢ Turn on the power.

6. ▢ Finish off with a hard rubber.
   ▢ Use a soft rubber to erase the errors.
   ▢ Brush or blow away the tiny rubber particles.

Unit 7 Workplace Interview

(Conversations 41 – 45)

An interview is a conversation between two people (the interviewer and the interviewee) where questions are asked by the interviewer to obtain information from the interviewee. An interview is the most valuable tool at Management's disposal for gathering information in the workplace. It provides an opportunity for the employee involved to explain his or her actions or opinions. Therefore, interviews usually take place at the workplace.

Conversation 41

> **Words and Expressions**
> single *a.* 单身的
> describe *v.* 描述
> personality *n.* 个性,性格
> hard-working *a.* 努力工作的
> eager *a.* 渴望的

(*Jill, the interviewer of a company, is interviewing Benson, one of the candidates.*)

Jill: Are you Benson Green?
Benson: Yes, I am.
Jill: Thank you for your coming.
Benson: Of course.
Jill: Would you like a cup of tea or coffee before we begin?
Benson: No, thanks. I'm fine.
Jill: All right. Then please come with me.
(*They both enter an office.*)
Jill: Please sit down. How are you doing this morning?
Benson: I'm doing fine. Thank you.
Jill: So, tell me a little bit about yourself.
Benson: Well. My name is Benson Green. I am 22 years old, and I am single.
Jill: How would you describe your personality[1]?
Benson: I'm hard-working, eager to learn. I enjoy working with other people. And I love meeting challenges[2].

Workplace Communication Skills 工作场所交流技能

1. How would you describe your personality? 请描述一下你的个性。
2. I love meeting challenges. 我喜欢接受挑战。

Questions:
1. How does Benson introduce himself?
2. How does Benson describe his personality?

Role-play:
Can you think of three more questions you might be asked at a job interview? Play Jack and Benson to continue the conversation.

Conversation 42

Words and Expressions
personal *a.* 个人的
alcoholic *n.* 酒鬼
behave *v.* 表现
envelope *n.* 信封
cheque *n.* 支票
generous *a.* 慷慨的
Las Vegas 拉斯维加斯

(*Tina is having serious personal problems. She is becoming an alcoholic and has started behaving badly. She is soon called into her boss's office and is told that she is being fired from her job.*)
Ben: Hi, Tina.
Tina: Hi, boss.
Ben: Good to see you ... Tina, we're going to let you go[1]. OK?
(*Ben hands Tina an envelope, Tina looks at the cheque inside.*)
Tina: This is too generous, Ben.
Ben: Well, Tina, we really liked having you around. But you know how it is[2].
Tina: I'm sorry.
Ben: Well, what are you going to do now?

Tina: I thought I'd move out to Las Vegas.

Notes:

1. Tom, we're going to let you go. 汤姆,我们准备让你离开了。
2. Well, Tom, we really liked having you around. But you know how it is. Tom,我们倒是喜欢让你在这里,可你知道是怎么回事。

Questions:

1. Who is Ben? Who is Tina?
2. Why does Ben want to see Tina?
3. Is it good news or bad news that Ben breaks to Tina?
4. How does Tina accept the news?
5. Do you think Ben handles the interview well? Why do you think so?

Conversation 43

Words and Expressions
career   *n.* 职业,前程
make good progress   进步很大
go along with   同意
package   *n.* 薪酬体系
salary   *n.* 薪水
company charge card   公司签账卡
expense account   公款支付账户

(*Diane is Edward's manager. Edward is talking with his manager about his career future.*)

Edward: Before I go, can we have a chat?
Diane: Sure. What about?
Edward: Diane, I have been with our company for 6 months now, and I'd like to talk about my future.
Diane: Is there a problem? Aren't you happy here?
Edward: Yes. But I would like to know what plans you have for me. I feel I've made good progress here over the last 6 months. What do you think?
Diane: I agree. We're very happy with what you have done. Of course you did make a few

mistakes, especially early on, but generally I see you as an important part of the team.

Edward: That's good to hear, thank you. I feel I've learned a lot here in the last 6 months. Obviously 6 months ago I couldn't have negotiated a large deal with our client ... but now I can[1].

Diane: Let's be open here[2], Edward. Are we talking about salary?

Edward: It's not just a question of money Diane. I want to look at the whole package. It's salary, performance-related bonus, a company charge card, an expense account, a car, and a more responsible position[3].

Diane: I think we should sit down, don't you?

(*to be continued*)

Notes:

1. I couldn't have negotiated a large deal with our client ... but now I can. 我不可能和客户去谈这么大的生意，……但现在我可以了。
2. Let's be open here: 我们还是有话直说吧。
3. I want to look at the whole package. It's salary, performance-related bonus, a company charge card, an expense account, a car, and a more responsible position. 我想谈整个薪酬包，包括工资、与业绩挂钩的奖金、公司签账卡、公款支付账户、汽车和一个更重要的职位。

Questions:
1. How long has Edward been working for the company?
2. What does Edward want to talk to Diane about?
3. What does Diane think of Edward's work performance?
4. What is the package Edward mentions in the conversation?
5. What exactly does Edward want to have?

Conversation 44

Words and Expressions
compromise   *n.* & *v.* 妥协，让步
bonus   *n.* 奖金
be worth   值得
make your targets   完成业务指标
precise   *a.* 精确的

> reach an agreement 达成一致
> be conditional on 以……作为条件
> negotiate v. 谈判

(*continued*)

Diane: Edward, if you insist on the car then I can't offer you such a large salary increase[1], and we'll have to find some compromise[2] on the performance-related bonus.
Edward: I think I am worth the salary[3].
Diane: I'm prepared to offer you a larger bonus, but if you accept that, you have to accept a smaller salary increase.
Edward: Could you be more precise[4]?
Diane: If you accept a fifteen percent increase in salary then I can add an extra five percent on that bonus figure. That represents a forty percent increase next year, if you fulfill your targets[5].
Edward: Okay, if you make that a seventeen percent salary increase, I think we can reach an agreement.
Diane: Good.
Edward: Which just leaves the matter of the car[6].
Diane: But Edward, I said the salary increase was conditional on your making a concession on the car[7].
Edward: I'll accept a smaller car.
Diane: All right. Now let's go through these points once more. Our boss is going to kill me[8]. Where did you learn to negotiate, Edward?
Edward: You taught me everything I know, Don.

Notes:

1. If you insist on the car then I can't offer you such a large salary increase. 如果你坚持要车，我就不能给你那么大的工资增幅。
2. find some compromise：找到双方都能妥协的地方。
3. I think I am worth the salary. 我认为我是值那份薪水的。
4. Could you be more precise? 你能不能说得更精确点？
5. That represents a forty percent increase next year, if you fulfill your targets. 如果你完成业务指标，这就表示明年会有40%的增加。
6. Which just leaves the matter of the car. 这就是说只剩下车的问题了。
7. the salary increase was conditional on your making a concession on the car：工资增长是以你在车的方面做出妥协为条件的。

8. Our boss is going to kill me. 我们老板会杀了我的。(玩笑话,意思是我给你的条件已经超出老板允许的范围了)

Questions:
1. On what condition does Diane agree to offer a large salary bonus?
2. Do they reach an agreement finally?
3. What agreement do they reach on car?
4. According to Diane, will her boss be happy about their agreement? Why?

Role-play:
You come to your boss's office to ask for a pay rise. Start a conversation following the outline below.

```
Start the conversation
         ↓
Talk about your performance
         ↓
Ask for a pay rise
         ↓
Finish the conversation
```

Conversation 45

Words and Expressions
vacancy   *n.* (职位)空缺
give thought to   考虑
take on   聘用
assistant   *n.* 助理
take on   雇佣
advertise   *v.* 做广告
internally   *adv.* 内部
applicant   *n.* 申请者
political   *a.* 政治的
promote   *v.* 提升
national   *a.* 全国的,国家的
policy   *n.* 政策

(*The HR manager, Andy, is talking with Lillian, his colleague, about the vacancy at their company.*)

Andy: So Lillian, have you given any more thought to taking on an assistant manager in marketing?

Lillian: Yes, but I'm still not sure about it. If we decided to take someone on, where would we advertise the vacancy?

Andy: Well, I guess we'd advertise the position internally as we always do.

Lillian: But if we advertised the job internally, we'd have the same old problems — not enough applicants and lots of internal political problems[1]. Could we advertise the job outside the company for once?

Andy: Well I suppose we could. But if we did, a lot of people wouldn't be very happy about it.

Lillian: Would that be a problem?

Andy: Well, yes. I mean, the company always talks about how we like to promote our own people and how you can develop a career with us[2]. So it'd look a bit funny if we didn't advertise it internally first[3].

Lillian: But even if we promoted one of our own people, the other internal applicants wouldn't be happy anyway. So what's the difference? Why couldn't we just advertise it in the national papers?

Andy: But it's company policy. You know that. We always advertise internally first.

Lillian: Yes, I know. But why can't we try something different for a change[4]? If we took someone on from outside the company, we'd bring some new ideas into the department. It's what we need.

Andy: Look, why don't we just advertise it internally as we always do, right? That'll keep everyone happy and then, after a couple of weeks, we can put an advertisement in the paper as well. What do you say?

Lillian: All right.

Notes:

1. But if we advertised the job internally, we'd have the same old problems — not enough applicants and lots of internal political problems. 但如果我们在公司内部招聘,就会出现老问题——应聘者不多,还会产生很多内部纷争。
2. The company always talks about how we like to promote our own people and how you can develop a career with us. 公司总是说我们如何提升员工,以及员工跟着我们会有前程。
3. So it'd look a bit funny if we didn't advertise it internally first. 如果我们这次不先在内部招聘,岂非有点可笑?
4. Why can't we try something different for a change? 我们为何不能试试不同方法改变一下呢?

Questions:
1. What does Lillian want to do with the job of taking on an assistant manager?
2. Does Andy agree with Lillian? Why?
3. What's the company policy? Why does the company have such a policy?
4. Do you agree with Lillian or Andy? Give your reasons.
5. What finally do they decide to do? Is it a good compromise?

Key Expressions

I. Talking with Boss
1. Can we have a chat?
2. I'd like to talk about . . .
3. I would like to know . . .
4. I feel/think that . . .
5. That's good to hear, thank you.
6. I want to look at . . .
7. Could you be more precise?
8. I'll accept . . .

II. Talking with an employee
1. What about?
2. Is there a problem?
3. Aren't you happy here?
4. I agree.
5. I see you as . . .
6. We're very happy with . . .
7. I'm prepared to . . .
8. If you accept . . . then I can . . .

Workshop

I. Business vocabulary.
1. Give the English version for the following business expressions.
   - (1) 努力工作的 _____
   - (2) 薪酬体系 _____
   - (3) 一张公司签账卡 _____
   - (4) 一个更加重要的职位 _____
   - (5) 绩效奖金 _____
   - (6) 完成业务目标 _____
   - (7) 以……作为条件 _____
   - (8) 空缺 _____
   - (9) 做广告 _____
   - (10) 雇佣 _____

2. Give the Chinese for the following business expressions.
   (1) make good progress _____
   (2) salary _____
   (3) an expense account _____
   (4) compromise _____
   (5) represent _____
   (6) reach an agreement _____
   (7) negotiate _____
   (8) assistant _____
   (9) applicant _____
   (10) promote _____

II. Translate the conversation into English.

Jodie：嗨，Helen，我就上周的会议来收集反馈意见的。你觉得这次的会议举办得怎么样？

Helen：嗯，还不错。每一部分都有趣，这次的演讲者也很不错。今年的会议比去年要好多了。我觉得与会者的人少一点就明显不一样。

Jodie：那么你觉得这次的酒店如何？

Helen：挺好。会议室大小适中，房间干净舒适。我挺喜欢这个酒店的。我觉得我们明年还应该去那。

Jodie：那你觉得周六的晚餐如何？

Helen：哦，那可能是这次唯一不好的地方。饭菜不是很好，服务也很慢。如果明年还去这个酒店，我们应该换一家餐馆。

III. Role play.

1. You are a new senior manager in a multinational company. You have to tell Mason, a long-serving middle manager, that there is no longer a position for him.
2. You are a sales manager and you are telling a salesman that he has not been doing well and that if he fails to fulfill his targets, he may not get any bonus by the end of the year.
3. Your internet start-up has just lost a large amount of money. You have to break the bad news to Mr. Black who has invested heavily in the business.

Part 2

Workplace Communication Skills

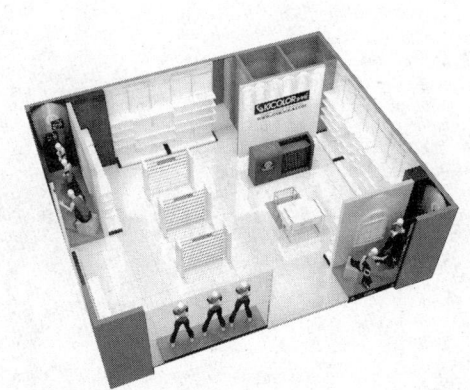

Unit 1 Verbal and Nonverbal Skills (1) *

Words and Expressions

verbal *a.* 语言的
denotation *n.* 本意,字面意思
connotation *n.* 言外之意,暗含意思
non-verbal *a.* 非语言的
inflection *n.* （音调）变化
posture *n.* 姿势,姿态
credibility *n.* 可信性,确实性
cue *n.* 提示,暗示
awkward *a.* 尴尬的
eliminate *v.* 消除,去除
prowess *n.* 勇敢,无畏
pitch *n.* 音调,音高
diction *n.* 措辞,用词
detract *v.* 减损,降低

Verbal communication consists of the spoken, as well as the written word. You can effectively express your message by using denotation, the dictionary meaning of a word, and connotation, the feelings associated with a word. Choosing exactly the right word increases the chances of your listener understanding the message you want to send. A common cause of misunderstanding during verbal communication is that our language constantly changes. New words are created and meanings of established words change with the generations and developments in technology[1].

Non-verbal communication can complement or contradict the spoken message[2]. The tone and inflection of the speaker's voice can emphasize the point, show conflict between what is spoken and what is meant[3], and reinforce the emotion of the message. Body language, such as eye contact and posture, can show interest or disinterest, welcome or warn, and reveal your level of confidence. Your appearance also communicates a message to listeners. If your attire or accessories are loud and distracting, they may take away from the effectiveness of your message[4]. Likewise, dressing appropriately and neatly adds to your credibility as a speaker.

A combination of verbal and non-verbal cues is a good strategy for effectively communicating your message. Smiling, laughing, and using a friendly tone of voice while saying, "That is so funny," lets your listener know that you really do think the situation is funny. However, making the same statement while using an unfriendly tone of voice accompanied by no smile, clearly lets your listener know that you do not, in fact, find the situation humorous. Pointing a finger in the direction you are describing is also an example of combining the verbal with the non-verbal for successful communication.

Learning to speak with authority and confidence can make you more successful in the workplace. Communicating with a trembling monotone voice[5] can send the message that you lack confidence and adequate social skills[6]. Although it can be difficult to develop strong communication skills, doing so can have a positive impact on both your business and personal interactions. Here are tips that will help you improve your verbal communication skills.

1. Think Before You Speak

Organizing your thoughts before speaking can reduce the amount of awkward pauses and verbal "hiccups[7]". It can also eliminate the need to make excessive amounts of clarifying statements[8]. Although it's not possible to make an outline for an impromptu dialogue[9], writing down your thoughts before planned discussions can improve your speaking prowess.

2. Use Direct and Concise Language

It's not necessary to use complex terminology to drive home important points[10]. Sometimes using complicated words and sentence structures can cause more confusion than it explains[11]. Avoid using "big words" to sound more educated because this can quickly backfire[12], unless you're sure of their usage and pronunciations.

3. Vary Your Vocal Tone

Express interest in what you're saying so others will pay attention to you. Use inflection to add emphasis to key phrases[13]. Raise and lower your pitch to express active emotion. Avoid blank stares[14] that stem from being bored.

4. Pronounce Words Completely and Correctly

Slow down when pronouncing difficult words to minimize mispronunciations. Practice your diction by recording yourself and analyzing the results. Don't use regional dialect as an excuse to continue making pronunciation errors[15]. Taking the time to correct deficiencies[16] can enhance your communication confidence and ability.

5. Master Your Nonverbal Communication Skills

Understand that your body language also has an effect on how your verbal communication is interpreted. Speaking with poor nonverbal cues such as slumping your shoulders or scowling[17] can detract from the effectiveness of your words. Stay in positive control of your body language to ensure your words are assessed correctly.

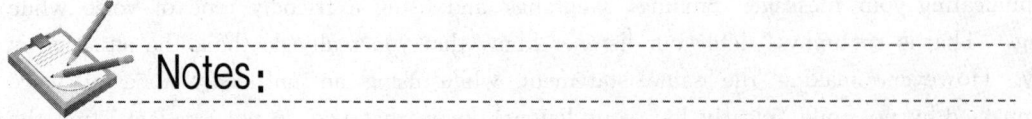

1. Meanings of established words change with the generations and developments in technology.

词汇的意思会随着一代代人的更替和科技的发展而产生变化。
2. complement or contradict the spoken message：对所说的话起补充或否定的作用。
3. show conflict between what is spoken and what is meant：说的和想的不一样。
4. If your attire or accessories are loud and distracting, they may take away from the effectiveness of your message. 如果你的服饰佩戴过于显眼惹人注目，就会影响你说话的效果。
5. a trembling monotone voice：颤抖单调的声音。
6. lack confidence and adequate social skills：缺乏自信和应有的社交技巧。
7. awkward pauses and verbal "hiccups"：尴尬的停顿和"呃呃"的声音。
8. clarifying statements：为澄清所做的表白。
9. make an outline for an impromptu dialogue：为即兴对话写一个提纲。
10. use complex terminology to drive home important points：用复杂的术语来解释重要观点。
11. Sometimes using complicated words and sentence structures can cause more confusion than it explains. 有时候使用复杂的词汇和句子，不但不能解释清楚，反而导致更多的混乱。
12. this can quickly backfire：很快显示出效果适得其反。
13. use inflection to add emphasis to key phrases：使用音调变化来强调关键词语。
14. blank stares：茫然的眼神。
15. Don't use regional dialect as an excuse to continue making pronunciation errors. 不要以地方方言为借口继续犯发音错误。
16. correct deficiencies：改正缺陷。
17. slumping your shoulders or scowling：肩膀下沉或愁眉苦脸。

Workshop

I. Decide whether the following statements are true or false according to the text.
1. Verbal communication consists of the spoken, as well as the written word. _____
2. Your appearance cannot communicate a message to listeners. _____
3. Dressing appropriately and neatly adds to your credibility as a speaker. _____
4. Communicating with a trembling monotone voice can send the message that you lack confidence. _____
5. You can use "big words" to sound more educated. _____
6. Understand that your body language also has an effect on how your verbal communication is interpreted. _____

II. Answer the following questions according to the text.
1. What is verbal communication? What is denotation? What is connotation?
2. What is nonverbal communication? Why is nonverbal communication important?
3. Why is it necessary to use a combination of verbal and non-verbal cues?
4. How can people improve their verbal communication skills?

III. Translate the following words or expressions.
1. nonverbal communication _____

2. connotation _____
3. credibility _____
4. enhance _____
5. pitch _____
6. 地域方言 _____
7. 即兴对话 _____
8. 社交技巧 _____
9. 改正缺陷 _____
10. 尴尬的停顿 _____

IV. Task:

People should adjust their use of voice in different situations. Please tell the strategy that each of the cases uses.

Situation 1. When a production manager raises his voice on the quality control of a new product, this shows his concerns for and also the importance of the new product.

Strategy: _____

Situation 2. When the speaker feels that his audience can understand him well, he can speak a little faster so as to make his words more lively and appealing.

Strategy: _____

Situation 3. Sometimes, the speaker may even pause for a few seconds when he raises a serious question. This will give the audience a chance to think the question over.

Strategy: _____

Unit 2　Verbal and Nonverbal Skills (2) *

> **Words and Expressions**
> signals　*n.* 信号,标志
> incongruent　*a.* 不一致的
> frown　*v.* 皱眉,不赞成
> concentrate　*v.* 集中
> animated　*a.* 活泼的,热烈的
> evade　*a.* 躲避,逃避
> confused　*a.* 困惑的,混乱的
> limp　*a.* 无力的,没精神的
> knack　*n.* 诀窍,窍门
> dramatically　*ad.* 戏剧性地

Good communication skills can help you in both your personal and professional life. While verbal and written communication skills are important, research has shown that nonverbal behaviors make up a large percentage of our daily interpersonal communication. How can you improve your nonverbal communication skills? The following top ten tips for nonverbal communication can help you learn to read the nonverbal signals of other people and enhance your own ability to communicate effectively.

1. Pay Attention to Nonverbal Signals

People can communicate information in numerous ways; so pay attention to things like eye contact, gestures, posture, body movements, and tone of voice[1]. All of these signals can convey important information that isn't put into words. By paying closer attention to other people's unspoken behaviors, you will improve your own ability to communicate nonverbally.

2. Look for Incongruent Behaviors

If someone's words do not match their nonverbal behaviors[2], you should pay careful attention. For example, someone might tell you they are happy while frowning and staring at the ground. Research has shown that when words fail to match up with nonverbal signals, people tend to ignore what has been said and focus instead on unspoken expressions of moods, thoughts, and emotions.

3. Concentrate on Your Tone of Voice When Speaking

Your tone of voice can convey a wealth of information, ranging from enthusiasm to disinterest to anger. Start noticing how your tone of voice affects how others respond to you and try using tone of voice to emphasize ideas that you want to communicate. For example, if you want to show genuine interest in something, express your enthusiasm by using an animated tone of voice.

4. Use Good Eye Contact

When people fail to look others in the eye, it can seem as if they are evading or trying to hide something. On the other hand, too much eye contact can seem confrontational or intimidating[3]. While eye contact is an important part of communication, it's important to remember that good eye contact does not mean staring fixedly into someone's eyes. How can you tell how much eye contact is correct? Some communication experts recommend intervals of eye contact lasting four to five seconds.

5. Ask Questions about Nonverbal Signals

If you are confused about another person's nonverbal signals, don't be afraid to ask questions. A good idea is to repeat back your interpretation of what has been said and ask for clarification[4]. An example of this might be, "So what you are saying is that . . ."

6. Use Signals to Make Communication More Effective and Meaningful

Remember that verbal and nonverbal communication work together to convey a message. You can improve your spoken communication by using body language that reinforces and supports what you are saying. This can be especially useful when making presentations[5] or when speaking to a large group of people.

7. Look at Signals as a Group

A single gesture can mean any number of things, or maybe even nothing at all. The key to accurately reading nonverbal behavior is to look for groups of signals that reinforce a common point[6]. If you place too much emphasis on just one signal out of many, you might come to an inaccurate conclusion about what a person is trying to communicate.

8. Consider Context

When you are communicating with others, always consider the situation and the context in which the communication occurs[7]. Some situations require more formal behaviors that might be interpreted very differently in any other setting. Consider whether or not nonverbal behaviors are appropriate for the context. If you are trying to improve your own nonverbal communication, concentrate on ways to make your signals match the level of formality necessitated by the situation[8].

9. Be Aware That Signals Can Be Misread

According to some, a firm handshake indicates a strong personality while a weak handshake is taken as a lack of fortitude[9]. This example illustrates an important point about the possibility of misreading nonverbal signals. A limp handshake might actually indicate something else entirely, such as arthritis[10]. Always remember to look for groups of behavior. A person's overall demeanor[11] is far more telling than a single gesture viewed in isolation.

10. Practice, Practice, Practice

Some people just seem to have a knack for using nonverbal communication effectively and correctly interpreting signals from others. These people are often described as being able to "read people." In reality, you can build this skill by paying careful attention to nonverbal behavior and practicing different types of nonverbal communication with others. By noticing nonverbal behavior and practicing your own skills, you can dramatically improve your communication abilities.

Notes:

1. tone of voice：声音的语调。
2. If someone's words do not match their nonverbal behaviors. 如果某人说的话与他们的非语言行为不匹配。
3. too much eye contact can seem confrontational or intimidating：过多的眼神接触会显得咄咄逼人或令人胆怯。
4. repeat back your interpretation of what has been said and ask for clarification：重复你对所说的话的理解并要求确认。
5. making presentations：进行演示。
6. look for groups of signals that reinforce a common point：寻找强调某一共同点的信号组。
7. always consider the situation and the context in which the communication occurs：永远要考虑沟通发生的场景和背景。
8. make your signals match the level of formality necessitated by the situation：让你的信号和情景要求的正规程度相匹配。
9. taken as a lack of fortitude：被认为缺少刚强。
10. A limp handshake might actually indicate something else entirely, such as arthritis. 一次软弱无力的握手可能表明完全无关的事情，比如关节炎。
11. A person's overall demeanor：一个人的整体举止。

Workshop

I. Decide whether the following statements are true or false according to the text.

1. While verbal and written communication skills are important, research has shown that nonverbal behaviors make up a large percentage of our daily interpersonal communication. _____

2. Things like eye contact, gestures, posture, body movements, and tone of voice can convey important information that isn't put into words. _____

3. If you want to show genuine interest in something, express your enthusiasm by using a boring tone of voice. _____

4. If you are confused about another person's nonverbal signals, don't be afraid to ask questions. _____
5. A firm handshake indicates a strong personality while a weak handshake is taken as a lack of fortitude. _____

II. Answer the following questions according to the text.
1. Why should we pay attention to nonverbal signals?
2. What does "incongruent behavior" mean?
3. Can you give examples showing the importance of "tone of voice"?
4. Why should we consider the situation and the context in communication?
5. What should we do to improve our nonverbal communication skills?

III. Translate the following words or expressions.
1. signals _____
2. frown _____
3. evade _____
4. tone of voice _____
5. knack _____
6. 眼神接触 _____
7. 共同点 _____
8. 缺乏毅力 _____
9. 整体举止 _____
10. 进行演讲 _____

IV. Tasks:

Task 1: Work in pairs. You meet for the first time at the airport. Greet each other and introduce yourselves according to the given information. Practice your nonverbal communication skill. Take cultural differences into consideration.

Student A: Your name is Mike. Your company is located in Sydney, Australia. You are the sales manager. Say that you are responsible for the business meeting and will be very pleased to help your guest during his stay in your city.

Student B: Your name is Liu. Your company is located in China. You come to the host company in Sydney for a business meeting. Say that you will stay there for five days and you are very happy to meet Mike. Thank him for his help.

Task 2: When two people meet, usually the one with a higher rank or authority will first extend his or her hand. Decide who should extend hands first in the following situations.

Situation 1:
    Peter Chang, male, employee in the sales department
    Mary Wang, female, a new comer to the sales department
    Generally speaking, _____ should extend his/her hand first.

Situation 2:
　　Mr. Lee, 29-year-old, employee in the customer service department
　　Mr. Jones, 40-year-old, employee in the personnel department
　　Generally speaking, _____ should extend his hand first.

Task 3: Analyze the following case and answer the questions.

　　An American went to an Arab country to meet his Arab counterpart for a business talk. The talk went on smoothly and both sides felt pleased.

　　At the break, both stood talking casually. As the Arab manager considered they knew each other quite well, he believed they should stand closer to show their closeness in their bilateral relationships. So he moved closer to the American manager. The American manager was surprised by the move. Then he thought maybe that action was unintentional. He showed no sigh in understanding the Arab's move, and just stepped back a bit to keep the distance.

　　On the Arab manager's part, he also felt surprised at the quiet stepping back by his American counterpart. He took it as a sign of ignorance of his good intention from that American manager. Therefore, he decided to move a step forward to show his sincerity.

　　Unfortunately, the Arab manager's furthered move make the American manager fell uncomfortable. However, as that was his first trip there, he did not want to spoil the nice talk by a trivial matter and make both sides embarrassed. So he quietly stepped back. This action was repeated several times until finally the American manager's back touched the wall — there was no more room for him to step back any further. Both the American and Arab managers felt frustrated by the situation, yet none of them could make out why the other side behaved like that.

Questions:
1. Why does the Arab manager change the distance with the American?
2. Why cannot the American manager accept the change?
3. What is your attitude towards cross-cultural differences? And what can you do to improve the situation?

Unit 3　Work Team Communication *

Words and Expressions
collaborate with　与……合作
one-time　*a.* 一时的
seminar　*n.* 讨论会,研讨班
interaction　*n.* 相互作用
luncheon　*n.* 午宴,正式的午餐会
objective　*n.* 目的,目标
appreciate　*n.* 感激,欣赏
familiarize　*v.* 使熟悉
image　*n.* 影像,形象
reinforcement　*n.* 加固,强化

At some point in your career, it's likely you'll have to collaborate with your coworkers on a project, goal or task. Whether it's a one-time event or a long-term arrangement, you'll need to learn how to communicate effectively and work well with your coworkers for the team effort to succeed. Being a successful team member demands good people skills, because you will have to draw upon the different backgrounds and skill-sets of your peers to get the job done[1].

A business team that uses effective communication techniques will see much more success than a team that lacks communication skills. Team communication should start with the manager — through training programs and seminars — and is one of the most important aspects of business success. Without the necessary communication skills, even the most talented and knowledgeable team member[2] probably won't see as much success as that of a less-talented, better communicator. Whether giving a presentation or listening to one of your coworkers talk in a meeting, several communication techniques will help you command respect, promote positivity and improve team success.

Step 1

Listen before speaking. The first and most important step in practicing effective business communication is paying close attention to what teammates say. Listening allows you time to think about what you will say, receive another perspective on a business matter[3] and earn respect from your teammates. Active listeners provide receptive nonverbal communication[4] through nodding, acknowledging comments, making eye contact and standing up straight, according to experts in nonverbal communication.

Step 2

Prepare for every interaction. Whether attending a business meeting, luncheon or private meeting with a teammate, it's important to know the subject matter of every meeting and be knowledgeable about it. Before every interaction, write down objectives, thoughts, questions and concerns about the topic. Your teammates and clients will appreciate your preparation and the meeting will operate much more efficiently.

Step 3

Brush up on your business writing skills[5]. Writing often doesn't receive the attention it deserves in business, but the average businessperson receives about 600 emails per week, and sends out hundreds[6]. The importance of writing warrants having a staff of good writers[7]. Whether you require team members to take a business writing class, or hire a professional for instruction, writing is essential in business.

Step 4

Practice proper etiquette[8]. Business etiquette extends far beyond the office[9]. Use it during every business interaction you attend. This includes presentations, meetings and business trips. Every business interaction has different rules, so familiarize yourself with a resource that clearly explains every etiquette point. Proper etiquette enhances your business image — one of the most important aspects of your career.

Step 5

Offer encouragement to teammates. Praise is an important part of business because it gives positive reinforcement, promotes team unity and keeps people working efficiently. If everything you say has a commanding and negative tone[10], the people around you will not be motivated to work as hard. Keep things positive and give people encouragement.

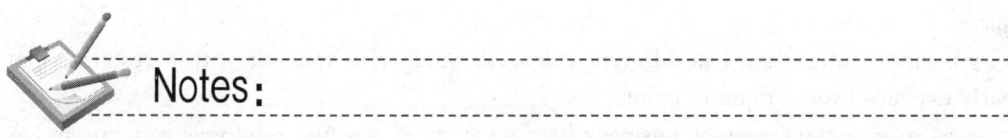

Notes：

1. draw upon the different backgrounds and skill-sets of your peers to get the job done：利用同事不同的背景和技能来完成工作。
2. most talented and knowledgeable team member：最有才华和见识的团队成员。
3. receive another perspective on a business matter：在商务问题上接受另一种看法。
4. provide receptive nonverbal communication：提供容易接受的非语言交流。
5. brush up on your business writing skills：重温你的商务写作技巧。
6. the average businessperson receives about 600 emails per week, and sends out hundreds：一个商务人士平均每周收到600封邮件，发出去上百封。
7. the importance of writing warrants having a staff of good writers：写作的重要性，使招聘善于写作的员工成为必要。
8. practice proper etiquette：运用恰当的礼仪。
9. business etiquette extends far beyond the office：商务礼仪的用途，远远不止在办公室。

10. a commanding and negative tone：命令和否定的语气。

Workshop

I. Complete the following sentences with the words given.

| arrangements | aspects | presentation | perspective |
| concern | luncheon | enhance | reinforcement |

1. I am sure that this meeting will contribute to the _____ of peace and security all over the world.
2. Climate and weather affect every _____ of our lives.
3. The staff is working frantically on final _____ for the summit.
4. He says the death of his father 18 months ago has given him a new _____ on life.
5. Earlier this month, a _____ for former U. N. staff was held in Vienna.
6. The White House is eager to protect and _____ that reputation.
7. The move follows growing public _____ over the spread of the disease.
8. James Watson, Philip Mayo and I gave a slide and video _____.

II. Translate the following sentences into Chinese.
1. Whether it's a one-time event or a long-term arrangement, you'll need to learn how to communicate effectively and work well with your coworkers for the team effort to succeed.
2. Whether giving a presentation or listening to one of your coworkers talk in a meeting, several communication techniques will help you command respect, promote positivity and improve team success.
3. Before every interaction, write down objectives, thoughts, questions and concerns about the topic.
4. Every business interaction has different rules, so familiarize yourself with a resource that clearly explains every etiquette point.
5. Praise is an important part of business because it gives positive reinforcement, promotes team unity and keeps people working efficiently.

III. Decide whether the following statements are T(ture) or F(false) based on the article.
1. You can always work independently and get succeed even without others' help. _____
2. A good team member should be capable of adapting to different cultures and getting along with people with varied religions and beliefs. _____
3. In business communication, speaking plays a much more important role than listening. _____
4. As a businessperson, sending and receiving mails is quite common. _____
5. Improper etiquette may ruin your business image and reputation. _____

Unit 4 Creating a Communication Climate

> **Words and Expressions**
> interact   v. 打交道,相互作用
> downcast   a. 垂头丧气的
> upbeat   a. 乐观的
> misjudge   v. 判断错误
> sustain   v. 保持
> subordinate   n. 下属
> pertain ... to   属于,关于,附属,适合
> diversity   n. 分歧,差异
> flexible   a. 灵活的
> exoneration   n. 赦免
> redemption   n. 赎回,偿还,补救

Communication climate is the emotional tone[1] of a relationship between people who are interacting. More specifically, it is the atmosphere of supportiveness or defensiveness that people feel within an organization[2]. Perhaps you feel downcast when the sky is overcast and feel upbeat when it's sunny. In much the same way as physical climates influence our moods, communication climates affect how people feel when they interact with one another. We feel on guard[3] when a supervisor blames us, a co-worker acts superior, someone flames us on the Internet[4], or a friend misjudges us. In each case, the communication climate is overcast.

In order to build and sustain a positive communication climate, we can consider the following guidelines.

1. Accept and Confirm Others[5]

Confirmation is a foundation of healthy communication climates. Each of us wants to feel valued, especially by those for whom we care most deeply. When communicators recognize, acknowledge, and endorse each other[6], they give the important gift of confirmation. They say, "You matter to me[7]." Although we can understand how important confirmation is, it isn't always easy to give it. Sometimes we disagree with others or don't like certain things they do. Communication research tells us that people expect real friends to give honest feedback, even if it isn't always pleasant to hear. Similarly, in the workplace managers, who give honest feedback, including criticism, are more likely to build strong working relationships with subordinates than managers who avoid criticism and conflict.

2. **Affirm and Assert Yourself**[8]

When learning effective ways of creating a good communication climate, it is once again important to know yourself. I believe it is important to be true to yourself so that you fight for your own beliefs in order to be individual[9] and to have respect for yourself. People need to accept the differences of others in order to be open to their feelings and cultural backgrounds. It is just as important to affirm and accept yourself as to do that for others. You are no less valuable than others, your needs are no less important, and your preferences are no less valid[10]. It is a misunderstanding to think that the interpersonal communication principles we've discussed concern only how we behave toward others. They pertain equally to how we should treat ourselves. Thus, the principle of confirming people's worth applies equally to others and ourselves[11]. This implies that you need to communicate your thoughts and feelings to give others a chance to confirm you.

3. **Respect Diversity Among People**

Just as individuals differ, so do relationships in personal and professional life. It's counterproductive to try to force all people and relationships to fit into a single mode[12]. We should strive to respect a range of communication choices and relationship patterns. In the workplace, it's important to understand that people vary widely in communication styles. To communicate effectively, we need to respect diversity among people. It's appropriate to ask others to explain behaviors that are not familiar to you. This lets them know that they matter to you, and it allows you to gain insight into different perspectives on interaction.

4. **Time Conflict Effectively**[13]

There are three ways to use timing so that conflicts are most likely to be civil and productive[14]. First, try to engage in conflict when every person is able to be fully present and mindful. Most of us are irritable when we are sick, tired, or stressed, so conflict is unlikely to be constructive. If time is limited or we are rushing, we're less likely to take the time to deal constructively with differences. Second, be flexible when you deal with differences. Constructive conflict is most likely when everyone's needs are accommodated[15]. If one person feels ready to talk about a problem, but the other doesn't, it's wise to delay discussion if possible. Of course, this works only if the person who is ready agrees to talk about the issue at a later time. A third way to use timing to promote positive conflict is bracketing, which marks off unessential issues for later discussion[16]. It lets us keep conflict focused productively[17]. Keep in mind, however, that bracketing works only when people actually do return to the issue they set aside.

5. **Show Grace When Appropriate**[18]

Although the idea of grace has not traditionally been discussed in communication texts, it is an important part of spiritual and philosophical thinking about ethical dimensions of human communication[19]. You don't have to be religious or know philosophy to show grace. All that's required is a willingness to sometimes excuse someone who has no right to expect your compassion or forgiveness[20]. None of us is perfect. We all make mistakes, hurt others with thoughtless acts, fail to meet responsibilities, and occasionally do things we know are wrong. Sometimes there is no reason others should forgive us when we wrong them; we have no right to expect exoneration. Yet human relations must have some room for redemption, for the extension of grace when it is not required or earned.

　　The guidelines we've discussed combine respect for self, others, relationships, and communication. Using these guidelines should enhance your ability to foster healthy affirming climates in your relationships with others.

Notes:

1. emotional tone：情调，感情色彩。
2. the atmosphere of supportiveness or defensiveness that people feel within an organization：人们在组织里感受到的支持或防卫的气氛。
3. We feel on guard：我们感到警惕。
4. a co-worker acts superior, someone flames us on the Internet：一个同事表现得高人一等，有些人在网上激怒我们。
5. accept and confirm others：接受和肯定他人。
6. recognize, acknowledge, and endorse each other：相互承认、肯定和支持。
7. You matter to me：你对我很重要。
8. affirm and assert yourself：肯定和坚持自己。
9. You fight for your own beliefs in order to be individual. 你为自己的信念战斗而成就自己的个性。
10. Your preferences are no less valid. 你的偏好没什么不合适的。
11. the principle of confirming people's worth applies equally to others and ourselves：肯定他人价值的原则可同样地用在别人和自己身上。
12. It's counterproductive to try to force all people and relationships to fit into a single mode. 试图强迫所有的人和关系去适合一种单独的模式，这是难以收效的。
13. time conflict effectively：有效把握（处理）冲突的时机。
14. civil and productive：文明和富有成效的。
15. Constructive conflict is most likely when everyone's needs are accommodated：每个人的需求都受到照顾时，建设性的解决冲突最有希望成为可能。
16. A third way to use timing to promote positive conflict is bracketing, which marks off unessential issues for later discussion：把握时机积极解决冲突的第三个方法是界定问题，也就是将不重要的枝节问题留待以后讨论。
17. keep conflict focused productively：将冲突集中在能产生积极效果的方面。
18. show grace when appropriate：在恰当的时候施加恩泽。
19. spiritual and philosophical thinking about ethical dimensions of human communication：关于人类交流伦理维度的精神和哲学思考。

20. a willingness to sometimes excuse someone who has no right to expect your compassion or forgiveness: 有时候愿意原谅那些没有权利指望你同情和原谅的人。

Workshop

I. Decide whether the following statements are true or false according to the text.

1. If you don't agree with people or feel the same way as they do, you have to insist your opinion. _____
2. Each of us is entitled to voice our thoughts, feelings, and needs. Accepting ourselves allows us to honor ourselves and to help others understand us. _____
3. We have to show our grace at any time. _____
4. A healthy communication climate will help employees avoid stress from conflict with co-workers. _____
5. There are four guidelines to help people create a healthy communication climate. _____
6. When you have conflict with others, you have to take a discussion immediately if you feel ready to talk about it. _____
7. In the workplace, it's important to understand that people vary widely in communication styles. _____

II. Answer the following questions according to the text.

1. Why do we have to create a communication climate?
2. What is a communication climate?
3. How many guidelines to help us create a communication climate?
4. What are the guidelines creating a communication climate?
5. How to time conflict effectively?

III. Case study.

  Alison was a new employee whom all of the customers loved for her deep knowledge of photography and willingness to teach customers on new and creative techniques. She had started to come in 5 - 10 minutes late regularly. James had been gently reminding her of the need for being on time nearly for a week now. After Alison had been there for about two months she started sitting while she took new photos from the picture-finishing unit. The first time James noticed this he mentioned it immediately, telling her, "Alison, we don't sit down while we're at work, especially where the customers can see you so easily." To which Alison replied, "I have to walk two miles just to get here from my apartment. Give me a break, OK?" Andy and Martha married five years ago when both completed graduate school. Last week Andy got the job offer of his dreams with one problem — he would have to move 1,500 miles away. Martha loves her current job and has no interest in moving or in living apart. Andy sees this job as one that could really advance his career. For the past week they have talked and argued continuously about the job offer. Tonight, while they are preparing dinner in their kitchen, they have returned to the topic once again. We join them mid-way in their discussion, just as it is heating up.

Andy: So today I was checking on the costs for flights from here to Seattle. If we plan ahead for visits, we can get round trip flights for around $300.00. That's not too bad.

Martha: While you're thinking about finances, you might consider the cost of renting a second apartment out there. We agreed last night that it would be too expensive to live apart.

Andy: I never agreed to that. Martha, can't you understand how important this job is to my career?

Martha: And what about our marriage? I suppose that's not important?

Andy: [He grabs a knife and begins cutting an onion] I never said that! If you'd pull with me on this, our marriage would be fine. You're just not ...

Martha: [She slams a pot on the stove.] Not what? Not willing to be the traditional supportive wife, I assume.

Andy: [He grimaces, puts down the knife, and turns to face Martha.] That isn't what I was going to say. I never asked you to be a traditional wife or to be anything other than who you are, but I want you to let me be myself too.

Martha: If you want to be yourself, then why did you get married? Marriage is about more than just yourself — it's about both of us and what's good for the two of us. You're not thinking of us at all.

Andy: And I suppose you are? You're only thinking about what you want. You don't seem to give a darn what I want. You're being incredibly selfish.

Martha: [She slams her hand against the counter and shouts.] Selfish?! I'm selfish to care about our marriage?

Andy: You're using that to manipulate me as if I don't care about the marriage and you do. If you really cared about it, maybe you'd consider moving to Seattle so we could be together.

Martha: [She raises her eyebrows and speaks in a sarcastic tone.] And just a minute ago you said you weren't asking me to be a traditional wife. Now you want me to be the trailing spouse so you can do what you please. Dandy!

Andy: I didn't say that. You're putting words in my mouth. What I said was ...

Martha: What you said was I should move to Seattle and support whatever it is you want to do.

Andy: [He slams the knife into the cutting board.] I did not say that. Quit telling me what I said! [He takes a deep breath, lowers his voice, then continues.] Look, Martha, can we just step back from this argument and try to look at the options with a fresh eye?

Martha: I've looked all I want to look. I've heard all I want to hear. You know where I stand on this, and you know I'm right even if you don't want to admit it.

Questions:

1. Identify examples of mindreading and describe their impact on Martha and Andy's discussion.
2. Identify communication that fosters a defensive interpersonal climate?
3. To what extent do you think Andy and Martha feel listened to by the other?

Unit 5 Working Together: Understanding Yourself and Others (1)

> **Words and Expressions**
> annoying   *a.* 令人讨厌的
> wavelength   *n.* 波长
> academic   *a.* 学术(界)的
> imaginative   *a.* 富于想象的
> spontaneity   *n.* 自发行为，自发性
> associate   *v.* (与)发生联系
> preference   *n.* 偏好，偏爱
> buzz   *n.* 嗡嗡声，乱哄哄的说话声
> extravert   *n.* 外向的人
> spectrum   *n.* 光谱，范围
> philosopher   *n.* 哲学家
> context   *n.* 情景，环境
> leaning   *n.* 倾向
> scary   *a.* 吓人的，可怕的
> logistics   *n.* 逻辑
> psychologist   *n.* 心理学家

Do you ever think that some colleagues are annoying? They seem not to be on your wavelength[1]. They deal with things very differently and you sometimes wonder how their mind works. If only you understood where they are coming from, working together could be so much easier. Personality plays a big role in how we view others, gather information, tackle problems, and organize our lives. Academic people often have quite similar personalities and this can lead to "blind spots"[2]. Imaginative people are often not good at the detail. Spontaneity is rarely associated with careful planning[3]. Once you understand different personalities, you can better understand your co-worker and yourself.

There are various ways of looking at personality, but one of the most popular and helpful is the Myers Briggs type indicator[4]. This system looks at our preferences on four different scales that explain why we often have difficulty understanding colleagues whose personalities differ significantly from our own.

1. Outgoing or a Reflective Thinker

There are those who prefer to solve their problems by talking them through[5], need other's company, are happy to work in open-plan, noisy situations[6]. It's the buzz of life that gives them their energy. Being the centre of attention and giving a lecture to a few hundred people is not a problem for them. Their energy is external and they are outgoing extraverts. People working in dramatic art and musicians are among those who often externalize their energy[7].

At the other end of this spectrum are those who prefer to reflect on issues, think things through thoroughly before discussing them. Their approach is more private and they like to be quiet. They are much more energized by reading a book than attending a party. At work they prefer an office of their own to open-plan situations. These are the reflective introverts[8]. Computer scientists, engineers and philosophers are sometimes among the most reflective thinkers.

At the extremes these two personalities can cause each other a lot of problems. Extraverts worry that introverts don't talk much and wonder what they think. Introverts just wish that extraverts would think first and talk when they have worked out their ideas.

Of course, we all behave differently in different contexts[9] but most of us have a leaning towards introversion or extraversion and this will affect our preferred way of doing things.

2. The Big Picture or Attention to Detail

The other day Jan Beery sent this picture to Katie Gutwein. She said, "One of the best images I've ever seen!" Katie responded coldly with "Unorganized ... scary!"

How opposite their reactions to a simple picture was! And how much does that tell you about them? Jan is very much a big picture person. She floats in the clouds and is constantly thinking of the next big wonder! She has a good overview of what is going on and a vision of what they want to achieve[10] but hate the detail. Katie on the other hand is very detail oriented[11]. How do we get this done, when is it due ... what are the logistics? She gets deeply involved in the details of a problem and neglects the big picture.

Myers Briggs calls the first "intuitive", the second "sensors"[12]. Intuitives have more imagination. Sensing types, by contrast, are most found among practical people — engineers, scientists and those involved in crafts. Their feet are firmly on the ground. They live in the present. They prefer to alter things step by step while "intuitives" want to change everything when put in charge[13].

Naturally "intuitives" believe that "sensors" are lacking in creativity and imagination while "sensors" think "intuitives" have their heads in the clouds[14]. Writers, journalists and psychologists tend to be above average on the intuitive side.

Notes:

1. They seem not to be on your wavelength. 他们与你观点不一。
2. this can lead to "blind spots": 这个会导致"盲点"(即不理解不同个性者的行为)。
3. spontaneity is rarely associated with careful planning: 率性而为绝少与周密计划联系在一起。
4. the Myers Briggs type indicator: 迈尔斯-布里格斯类型指标(简称 MBTI)。美国的凯恩琳·布里格斯和她的女儿伊莎贝尔·布里格斯·迈尔斯研制了迈尔斯-布里格斯类型指标(MBTI)。这个指标以瑞士心理学家荣格划分的 8 种类型为基础,加以扩展,形成四个维度,即:① 外倾(E)—内倾(I);② 直觉(N)—感觉(S);③ 思维(T)—情感(F);④ 判断(J)—知觉(P)。四个维度如同四把标尺,每个人的性格都会落在标尺的某个点上,这个点靠近哪个端点,就意味着个体就有哪方面的偏好。如在第一维度上,个体的性格靠近外倾这一端,就偏外倾,而且越接近端点,偏好越强。
5. solve their problems by talking them through: 通过讨论来解决问题。
6. work in open-plan, noisy situations: 在公开讨论和嘈杂的情景中工作。
7. externalize their energy: 将他们的精力外化。
8. reflective introverts: 爱沉思的、性格内向的人
9. behave differently in different contexts: 在不同的情景下有不同的行为。
10. She has a good overview of what is going on and a vision of what they want to achieve. 她对于正在发生的事情能很好把握,对他们想得到的东西看得很清楚。
11. detail oriented: 关注细节的。
12. Myers Briggs calls the first "intuitives", the second "sensors". 迈尔斯·布里格斯把第一种人称为"直觉者",把第二种人称为"感觉者"。
13. when put in charge: 在主管的位置。这是一种省略,等于 when they are put in charge。
14. have their heads in the clouds: 头在云雾里,不着边际。

Workshop

I. Decide whether the following statements are true or false according to the text.

1. Personality differences are common in the workplace. _____
2. Myers Briggs type indicator has five different scales. _____
3. "Intuitives" prefer to alter things incrementally while "sensors" put them in charge and they want to change everything. _____
4. Writers, journalists and psychologists tend to be above average on the analytical side. _____
5. Introverts just wish that extraverts would think first and talk when they have worked out their ideas. _____
6. Once you understand personalities, you will find out just how many people don't have any understanding. _____

II. Answer the following questions according to the text.

1. What is Myers Briggs type indicator?
2. What types are included in Myers Briggs type indicator?
3. Why do we need to understand different types of personalities?
4. What are "intuitives" and "sensors"?
5. What are introverts?
6. What can lead to "blind points"?

III. Put the following words and expressions into Chinese.

1. Reflective thinker _____
2. Get involved in _____
3. Intuitives have more imagination _____
4. They seem not to be on your wavelength _____
5. detail oriented _____
6. blind spot _____

Unit 6　Working Together: Understanding Yourself and Others (2)

> **Words and Expressions**
> analytical　*a.* 分析的
> deduce　*v.* 推断
> detached　*a.* 保持距离的
> objective　*a.* 客观的
> subjective　*a.* 主观的
> illogical　*a.* 不合逻辑的,没有逻辑的
> flexible　*a.* 灵活的
> freak　*n.* 怪人,怪胎

1. Analytical or People Based Solutions

Scientists and mathematicians approach problem solving by deducing from first principles[1]. They start somewhere and work logically towards a correct solution. Provided the logic is good, the answer must be right. But will people accept it? "Thinkers" who work this way do the logic first and sell the solution to others later. Most, but not all, scientists and engineers are strongly analytical.

The "feeling" method is to consider what kind of solution people want and start from there. Those using this approach tend to solve a problem as though they were part of it while analysts are able to be much more detached. One is objective and the other subjective. Analysts think subjective problem solvers are illogical. The clergy and those in social work are often strongly "feeling" problem solvers[2]. They may find analysts cold and unfeeling. If you're in an academic department where you are supposed to be logical, but your approach is different, that will cause problems, and vice versa[3].

2. Judging or Perceiving[4]

Do you plan, organize and think ahead? Some of us like to be in control. They have to do lists and diaries[5]. They plan their day, their week and year. Holidays are usually booked well in advance and perhaps they like them to be structured. Myers Briggs calls these "Judging" types. With tidy desks and offices they know exactly where to find things, whether at work or at home. Others, she calls "Perceiving", feel hemmed in if their life is organized a month ahead[6]. They prefer to go with the flow[7], work flexible hours, take life as it comes and be ready for new experiences[8].

At one end of this particular type are the control freaks[9]. At the other they are much more laid back[10]. "Judging" types finish their work before taking their leisure; "Perceiving" types are ready for leisure pursuits[11] now. If your boss is the opposite type to you in this particular category it will be an interesting relationship.

Understanding others' personalities doesn't mean fixing them or correcting them[12]. It means knowing how to best respond to them and approach them. If you know that your boss is a sensor, then paying attention to details is a good way to make him happy.

Once we understand the different personalities, it is much easier to accept them. You will know that you cannot change someone's personality, just like you wouldn't want to change yours. Acceptance helps to know where to step and what to avoid[13].

Getting along with personalities goes a step further. Once you understand and accept them, you have to do your best to get along with them. In your life there is a good chance that you have come across a personality conflict[14]. If you knew the right way to deal with the situation then it wouldn't have become a conflict.

To get to this point is going to take some work[15]. You are going to have to study people and try to understand them. You are also going to have to look critically at yourself[16] and try to improve your weaknesses and keep your strengths in check[17].

Once you understand personalities, you will find out just how many people don't have any understanding. When these people do or say something that offends you, remember not to look too deep into it, they just don't understand your personality. When this happens, you are able to avoid a conflict thanks to your understanding.

Notes:

1. deducing from first principles：从基本原理中进行推断。
2. The clergy and those in social work are often strongly "feeling" problem solvers. 牧师和社会工作者经常是些十分依仗感觉来解决问题的人。
3. vice versa：反之亦然。
4. judging or perceiving：判断型还是感觉型。
5. They have to do lists and diaries. 他们非得列清单，写日记。
6. feel hemmed in if their life is organized a month ahead：如果生活在一个月前就计划好了，他们会觉得备受束缚。
7. go with the flow：随大流。
8. take life as it comes and be ready for new experiences：顺其自然，准备接受新的经历。
9. control freaks：控制狂。
10. at the other they are much more laid back：处于另一端的人则要放松得多。
11. ready for leisure pursuits：做好玩的准备。
12. Understanding others' personalities doesn't mean fixing them or correcting them. 懂得他人的个性并不表示要修理或纠正他们。
13. Acceptance helps to know where to step and what to avoid. 接受（他人的个性）让你知道什么地方可以前进，什么地方需要避让。
14. There is a good chance that you have come across a personality conflict. 你很可能会碰上个

性冲突。
15. To get to this point is going to take some work. 到达这一步要做些工作。
16. look critically at yourself：批评地看待自己。
17. improve your weaknesses and keep your strengths in check：弱点要改进，长处要控制。

Workshop

I. Decide whether the following statements are true or false according to the text.
1. "Judging" type of people feel hemmed in if their life is organized a month ahead. _____
2. If we understand others' personalities, we can fix them or correct them. _____
3. Most, but not all, scientists and engineers are strongly analytical. _____
4. Scientists and mathematicians are often strongly "feeling" problem solvers. _____
5. "Judging" prefers to go with the flow, work flexible hour. _____
6. "Perceiving" types are ready for leisure pursuits. _____

II. Answer the following questions according to the text.
1. How to understand perceiving?
2. How do scientists and mathematicians approach problem solving?
3. How does perceiving feel if their life is organized a month ahead?
4. What should you do when these people do or say something that offends you?
5. What type of people would think subjective problem solvers are illogical?
6. What type of people would like to be in control?

III. Put the following words and expressions into Chinese.
1. getting along with personalities _____
2. leisure pursuits _____
3. look critically at yourself _____
4. vice versa _____
5. control freaks _____
6. go with the flow _____
7. take life as it comes _____

IV. Determine each person's type of personality.
1. Lisa has high energy. Generally, she acts first and then thinks. She's quite outgoing and enthusiastic. She prefers to do a lot of things at once, but she can be easily distracted sometimes. _____
2. Monica often take many things personally. If she gets appreciation, she is quite motivated; if she gets blamed, she will turn upset soon and demotivated. _____
3. Linda admires creative ideas. she focuses on big pictures and possibilities. she trusts her gut instinct a lot. _____
4. When Susan needs to make decision, she often makes it pretty quickly. She prefers to work first and play later. She finds comfort in schedules. _____

5. Thomas likes staying at home rather than joining parties. When he wants to do something, he thinks first and then acts. He prefers to focus one thing at a time. _____

V. Case study.

1. Mike Link asks you to come into his office. You know that he is upset about his arrangement for his meeting this morning — the overhead projector's bulb burned out, there weren't enough chairs in the meeting room, the reports copied for the meeting were out of order, and the refreshments arrived an hour late. As you enter, he asks you to sit down and he gets right to the issue at hand, saying: "You've got to do something about improving quality of your work, your dependability and the way you communicate. So what are you going to do to make these things better?" What is the most effective way to respond and communicate with Mike?

2. Mary Gerard, one of your co-workers, is known as the "socialize". You arrive early Friday morning to get a head start on a project that's due by 10 a.m. Mary stops by your desk and starts talking about the party she's throwing that night and who may stop by. What you thought would be a few minutes turns into a half hour. Your supervisor walks by and gives you the "evil eye". The pressure is on and you must finish your project. How do you get Mary to leave without hurting her?

Workplace Communication Skills 工作场所交流技能

Unit 7 Conducting Meetings

> **Words and Expressions**
> participation　*n.* 参加，参与
> venue　*n.* 会场，活动地点
> agenda　*n.* 会议议程
> minutes　*n.* 会议记录
> proceed　*v.* 继续进行
> dominate　*v.* 支配，控制
> step in　插手帮助(干预)，介入
> in advance　提前，事先

Most organizations use meetings in the course of their work, and these meetings can be successful or unsuccessful, depending on whether they are managed properly. Managers must learn to properly organize and conduct meetings to contribute to organizational effectiveness[1]. There are several important principles to conduct meetings, which are described as follows.

1. Planning and Preparation

Planning should improve participation by ensuring that that the members are well prepared for the meeting. This is the responsibility of the chairperson, secretary and executive[2], depending on the type of organization.

Planning does not mean controlling and directing the meeting in such a way that it restricts participation[3]. Normally, you will have to do the following things when you plan and prepare for a meeting:

— Identify one or more topics.
— Identify the people who will be asked to attend the meeting.
— Identify a time, date and venue.
— Create paperwork to invite people to the meeting.

— Prepare a list of topics to be discussed (an agenda).

— Prepare your own input for the meeting, which should be relevant to the purpose of the meeting.

— Create paperwork to record the outcome of the meeting (minutes).

It is the organizer's responsibility to ensure that everyone has been notified of the date, time and venue of the meeting, as well as the main issues to be discussed. For many organizations it is a useful practice to always have their meetings on the same day and in the same place. This will help you to cut costs, and to make sure that everyone knows where they can find the meeting.

2. Follow the Plan

You should follow the plan for the meeting item by item. In most meetings the discussion tends to stray and new items tend to come up[4]. As leader, you should keep the discussion on track[5]. If new items come up during the meeting, you can take them up at the end — or perhaps postpone them to a future meeting.

3. Move the Discussion Along

As a leader, you should control the agenda. When one item has been covered, bring up the next item. When the discussion moves off subject, move it back on subject[6]. In general, do what is needed to proceed through the items efficiently. But you should not cut off discussion before all the important points have been made. Thus, you will have to use your good judgment. Your goal is to permit complete discussion on the one hand and to avoid repetition, excessive details, and useless comments[7] on the other.

4. Control Those Who Talk too Much

Keeping certain people from talking too much is likely to be one of your harder tasks. A few people usually tend to dominate the discussion. Your task as leader is to control them. Of course, you want the meeting to be democratic, so you will let these people talk as long as they are contributing to the goals of the meeting. However, when they begin to stray, duplicate, or bring in useless matter[8], you should step in. You can do this tactfully and with all the decorum of business etiquette[9] by asking for other viewpoints or by summarizing the discussion and moving on to the next topic.

5. Encourage Participation from Those Who Talk Too Little

Just as some people talk too much, some talk too little. In business groups, those who say little are often in positions lower than those of other group members. Your job as leader is to encourage these people to participate by asking them for their viewpoints and by showing respect for the comments they make, even though the comments may be illogical.

6. Control Time

When your meeting time is limited, you need to determine in advance how much time will be needed to cover each item. Then, at the appropriate time, you should end discussion of the items. You may find it helpful to announce the time goals at the beginning of the meeting and to remind the group members of the time status during the meeting.

7. Summarize at Appropriate Place

After a key item has been discussed, you should summarize what the group has covered and concluded. If a group decision is needed, the group's vote will be the conclusion. In any event[13], you should formally conclude each point and then move on to the next one. At the end of the meeting, you can summarize the progress made. For some formal meetings, minutes kept by a secretary provide a summary.

8. How to Write Minutes

The minutes of a meeting can be very different in style and detail. The following information should be included:

— Nature of meeting, date, time venue.
— Names of those present.
— Names of visitors.
— Summaries of decisions and discussions.

This includes work to be followed up and who have taken responsibility for certain tasks. The minutes should be written neatly in a special minute book or file. The book or file should be kept safely and always available for consultation at any time[10]. The following is a sample minutes for a meeting:

Subject: New office equipment
Date: 19 April 2012
Participants: JS, KG, EDG, CBM, DG

Agenda Item	Decision	Reason	Action
1. Change computer supplier	Agreed	Present supplier too expensive	CBM to check companies by 15/5
2. New chairs	Agreed	Staff have back problems	JS to buy by 15/5
3. Take out walls	Not agreed	Difficult to work; too much noise from colleagues	None
4. Install coffee bar on the 6th floor	Agreed	Improve communication and atmosphere	DG to check costs by 15/5

 Notes:

1. contribute to organizational effectiveness: 提高组织效率。

2. the responsibility of the chairperson, secretary and executive：会议主持人，秘书和执行官的职责。
3. controlling and directing the meeting in such a way that it restricts participation：以限制与会者的方式来控制和指导会议。
4. the discussion tends to stray and new items tend to come up：谈论往往会偏离主题，而且会出现新的议题。
5. keep the discussion on track：使讨论不偏题。
6. When the discussion moves off subject, move it back on subject. 当谈论偏离主题时，将其转移回来。
7. avoid repetition, excessive details, and useless comments：避免重复、过多的细节和无益的评论。
8. When they begin to stray, duplicate, or bring in useless matter. 当他们开始离题、重复或者谈论不相干的事情时。
9. You can do this tactfully and with all the decorum of business etiquette. 你可以巧妙地做到这一点，并完全符合商务礼仪。
10. available for consultation at any time：随时可供查阅。

Workshop

I. Decide whether the following statements are true or false according to the text.

1. Planning means running the meeting in such a way that it restricts participation. _____
2. An agenda should be short, simple and clear. _____
3. The agenda is a list of issues for participants to discuss. _____
4. "Decide or confirm time and place for next meeting" should be stated on the agenda. _____
5. As a leader, when the discussion move off subject, you should not cut off discussion to keep it on track. _____
6. In business groups, those who are in lower position should be ignored. _____
7. It is no use announcing the time goals at the meeting and remind the group members of the time status during the meeting. _____
8. The minutes can be written either in a special minute book or file or on scraps of paper. _____

II. Answer the following questions according to the text.

1. What will we have to do when we plan and prepare for a meeting?
2. Why should we set an agenda?
3. How can we step in when some people begin to stray, duplicate, or bring in useless matter?
4. What should we summarize at the end of the meeting?
5. What items should be covered in the minutes of a meeting?
6. Can you add more tips as advice for holding effective meetings?

III. Reflection.

Read the following sample of minutes and compare it with the one in the passage. Which one do you prefer? Why?

Minutes of a Monthly Meeting of Board of Directors

Time: June 5th, 2012, 2:30 p.m.

Place: Meeting Room, fifth floor, the Central Building of Garden Hotel

Participants: All the directors

Chairman: Chairman of the board, Mr. Johnson

Minutes keeper: Lucy

The chief items at the meeting:

After the meeting was declared open, Mr. Johnson, chairman of the board, made a report on the work and total sales of the company at this season, which was followed by a heated discussion.

All the directors agreed to hold a press conference for the company next month and suggested inviting experts from America to give a training course to all the employees of the company.

The meeting adjourned at 5:30 p.m.

IV. Case Study.

The CFO is a meeting addict. He calls meetings 2-3 times a week and they can last for hours mainly because there are so many participants and there is no formal agenda. Or if there is an agenda, they somehow get way off track. His group is starting to dread a meeting before it starts for fear of missing lunch and even dinner. How can I help him be more organized?

Questions:

1. What are the problems with the meetings in this situation?
2. If you were the author, what would you suggest to improve?

Unit 8 Dealing with Conflict

Words and Expressions

conflict *n.* 冲突
animosity *n.* 敌意
surface *n.* 表面
spiral *n.* 螺旋形（上升或下降）
exploit *v.* 利用
bruise *v.* 使碰伤
collaborative *a.* 合作的
assertive *a.* 自信的，坚持的
compromising style 妥协方式
relinquish *v.* 放弃
at a standstill 停顿
accommodator *n.* 适应者
overall *ad.* 总体上
evade *v.* 逃避
default *n.* 违约、拖欠
hostility *n.* 敌对状态

In many cases, conflict in the workplace just seems to be a fact of life[1]. We've all seen situations where different people with different goals and needs have come into conflict. And we've all seen the often-intense personal animosity[2] that can result.

The fact that conflict exists, however, is not necessarily a bad thing: As long as it is resolved effectively, it can lead to personal and professional growth. In many cases, effective conflict resolution can make the difference between positive and negative outcomes[3].

The good news is that by resolving conflict successfully, you can solve many of the problems that it has brought to the surface, as well as getting benefits that you might not at first expect[4].

1. **Increased Understanding**

The discussion needed to resolve conflict expands people's awareness of the situation, giving them an insight into how they can achieve their own goals without undermining those of other people.

2. **Increased Group Cohesion**[5]

When conflict is resolved effectively, team members can develop stronger mutual respect and a renewed faith[6] in their ability to work together.

3. Improved Self-knowledge

Conflict pushes individuals to examine their goals in close detail, helping them understand the things that are most important to them, sharpening their focus[7], and enhancing their effectiveness.

However, if conflict is not handled effectively, the results can be damaging. Conflicting goals can quickly turn into personal dislike. Teamwork breaks down[8]. Talent is wasted as people disengage from their work. And it's easy to end up in a vicious downward spiral of negativity and recrimination[9].

If you're to keep your team or organization working effectively, you need to stop this downward spiral as soon as you can. To do this, it helps to understand different styles people use to deal conflict.

Understanding the Theory: Five Styles for Conflict Resolution

In the 1970s Kenneth Thomas and Ralph Kilmann identified five main styles of dealing with conflict that vary in their degrees of cooperativeness and assertiveness[10]. They argued that people typically have a preferred conflict resolution style[11]. However they also noted that different styles were most useful in different situations. They developed the Thomas-Kilmann Conflict Mode Instrument which helps you to identify which style you tend towards when conflict arises.

1. Competitive

People who tend towards a competitive style take a firm stand, and know what they want. They usually operate from a position of power, drawn from things like position, rank, expertise, or persuasive ability[12]. This style can be useful when there is an emergency and a decision needs to be make fast; when the decision is unpopular; or when defending against someone who is trying to exploit the situation selfishly. However it can leave people feeling bruised, unsatisfied and resentful when used in less urgent situations.

2. Collaborative

People tending towards a collaborative style try to meet the needs of all people involved. These people can be highly assertive but unlike the competitor, they cooperate effectively and acknowledge that everyone is important. This style is useful when you need to bring together a variety of viewpoints to get the best solution; when there have been previous conflicts in the group; or when the situation is too important for a simple trade-off[13].

3. Compromising

People who prefer a compromising style try to find a solution that will at least partially satisfy everyone. Everyone is expected to give up something and the compromiser him or herself also expects to relinquish something. Compromise is useful when the cost of conflict is higher than the cost of losing ground[14], when equal strength opponents are at a standstill and when there is a deadline looming.

4. Accommodating

This style indicates a willingness to meet the needs of others at the expense of the person's own needs. The accommodator often knows when to give in to others, but can be persuaded to surrender a position even when it is not warranted[15]. This person is not assertive but is highly cooperative. Accommodation is appropriate when the issues matter more to the other party, when peace is more valuable than winning, or when you want to be in a position to collect on this "favor" you gave. However people may not return favors, and overall this approach is unlikely to give the best outcomes.

5. Avoiding

People tending towards this style seek to evade the conflict entirely. This style is typified by delegating controversial decisions[16], accepting default decisions, and not wanting to hurt anyone's feelings. It can be appropriate when victory is impossible, when the controversy is trivial, or when someone else is in a better position to solve the problem. However in many situations this is a weak and ineffective approach to take.

Friction in the workplace can be stressful and counterproductive for everyone involved. Apart from the big theoretical strategies mentioned above, it is also important to learn to approach the person with whom you are struggling to resolve the situation. You may follow these few steps to alleviate awkwardness in the workplace[17].

(1) Decide whether you want to confront the person who is bothering you. It is usually better to air grievances in the open than to let them fester[18].

(2) Speak to the other person calmly, politely and rationally. Focus on the situation and facts, avoiding gossip and personal attacks.

(3) Be careful not to express hostility in your posture, facial expression or tone. Be assertive without being aggressive[19].

(4) Listen to the other person carefully: What is he/she trying to say? Be sure you understand his/her position.

(5) Express interest in what the other person is saying. You can acknowledge her ideas without necessarily agreeing or submitting. Saying, "I understand that you feel this way. Here's how I feel ..." acknowledges both positions.

(6) Communicate clearly what you want, offering positive suggestions and recommendations. Be willing to be flexible.

(7) Speak to your supervisor if a problem with a difficult co-worker seriously threatens your work, but avoid whining[20].

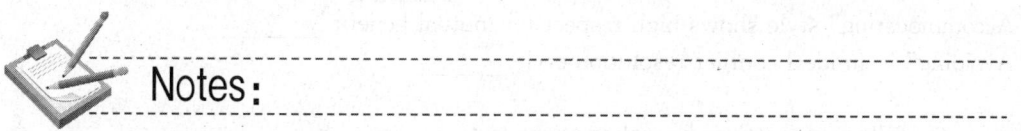

Notes:

1. conflict in the workplace just seems to be a fact of life: 冲突在工作场所无疑是家常便饭。
2. often-intense personal animosity: 经常是强烈的个人敌意。

3. effective conflict resolution can make the difference between positive and negative outcomes：有效地解决冲突，结果便有好坏之分。
4. getting benefits that you might not at first expect：获得始未预料的好处。
5. increased group cohesion：增强群体凝聚力。
6. stronger mutual respect and a renewed faith：相互之间更为尊重，更为信任。
7. sharpening their focus：使关注度更加集中。
8. teamwork breaks down：团队分崩离析。
9. to end up in a vicious downward spiral of negativity and recrimination：结果陷入互相否定和指责的恶性循环。
10. five main styles of dealing with conflict that vary in their degrees of cooperativeness and assertiveness：有五种解决冲突的主要方式，它们在与对方合作或坚持己见方面程度各有不同。
11. people typically have a preferred conflict resolution style：人们通常都有自己偏好的解决冲突的方式。
12. operate from a position of power, drawn from things like position, rank, expertise, or persuasive ability：（行事）从实力出发，这一实力源于职位、级别、专业能力或说服能力。
13. the situation is too important for a simple trade-off：事情太重要，不能搞简单的交易。
14. the cost of conflict is higher than the cost of losing ground：冲突的代价高于放弃立场的代价。
15. surrender a position even when it is not warranted：在并无必要时放弃立场。
16. delegating controversial decisions：下达有争议的决策。
17. alleviate awkwardness in the workplace：缓和工作场所出现的尴尬。
18. it is usually better to air grievances in the open than to let them fester：将不满公开通常比让其加剧好。
19. be assertive without being aggressive：果断而不咄咄逼人。
20. avoid whining：不要哭哭啼啼。

Workshop

I. Decide whether the following statements are true or false according to the text.

1. Conflict in the workplace is very seldom. _____
2. Generally speaking, conflict in the workplace is a bad thing, and it cannot lead to any good result. _____
3. According to Kenneth Thomas and Ralph Kilmann, there are four main conflict resolution styles. _____
4. "Competitive" is an agreeable, non-assertive style. _____
5. "Accommodating" style shows high respect for mutual benefit. _____
6. "Avoiding" is an ideal conflict resolution style. _____

II. Answer the following questions according to the text.

1. Why is the conflict at work not necessarily a bad thing?
2. What are the benefits that the conflict at work can yield?

3. What are the advantages of "collaborative" style of dealing with conflict?
4. What are the features of each style of dealing with conflict?
5. According to the passage, what are the suggestions to alleviate the awkwardness at work?

III. Determine each person's style of conflict resolution.
1. Adriana believes she is the best accountant in the company. Whenever there is a conflict in the workplace, she always thinks she is right. _____
2. Pedro is a new employee. He will do any job he is asked to do without question even if it interferes with the work he is responsible for. _____
3. Sue has worked in the company for many years. She loves her current job. Whenever there is conflict at work, she is always helpful. She can deal with conflict effectively. _____
4. Henri does not want to face the conflict directly, if there is conflict, he always avoid it by asking for leave. _____
5. Whenever there is a conflict at work, Mike tends to give up something so that both parties can meet each other half way. _____

IV. Case study.
James had been a manager at XYZ Photo Shop for 4 years. James' management style was to create a comfortable environment for employees. Besides the basic requirements, James set only two rules: he demanded that the employees should be on time and did not allow employee to sit down in an area where customers were shopping.

Alison was a new employee whom all of the customers loved for her deep knowledge of photography and willingness to teach customers on new and creative techniques. She had started to come in 5 – 10 minutes late regularly. James had been gently reminding her of the need for being on time nearly for a week now. After Alison had been there for about two months she started sitting while she took new photos from the picture-finishing unit. The first time James noticed this he mentioned it immediately, telling her, "Alison, we don't sit down while we're at work, especially where the customers can see you so easily." To which Alison replied, "I have to walk two miles just to get here from my apartment. Give me a break, OK?"

Questions:
1. James has a competent employee and dislikes the thought of hiring and training new employees. However, he can't simply allow employees to violate the set rules. What should he do to deal with the conflict?
2. If you were James, how would you communicate with Alison in order to deal with the conflict at work?